Twayne's United States Authors Series

Sylvia E. Bowman, *Editor*

INDIANA UNIVERSITY

Bernard Malamud

BERNARD MALAMUD

by SIDNEY RICHMAN
California State College at Los Angeles

 109

Twayne Publishers, Inc. :: New York

813
R

FOR ESTELLE, LESLEY, AND ADAM

Preface

THIS BOOK is quite frankly intended as an introductory study—a novel-by-novel, story-by-story analysis—which will supply the reader with as thorough an exposure to Malamud's fiction as space allows. The difficulties inherent in dealing with an author whose career is still prospering and whose art is continually being refashioned under the stress of new techniques are perhaps obvious; but a few of them are worth recounting for the effect they have had in shaping both the content and the tone of this study.

Perhaps the severest limitation is the realization that almost everything that is to be said about Malamud's underlying intentions as well as his achievements had to be extracted from a close study of the fiction itself. Although Malamud is generally considered one of America's most important new writers, he has not yet attracted that community of scholarly evaluation which surrounds either a completed or a lengthy career and from which one can draw for guidance and authority. For another, it seems obvious that whatever direction might be derived from biographical interpretation, such an approach would have to wait for later and ampler studies. The data for such a study was too sparse to be truly illuminating, and in any case its use seemed premature, if not unseemly.

Added to these is another and a greater difficulty: the realization that most of my conclusions are doomed to tentativeness. A writer's career is constantly and totally in motion, and each new impulse and change of direction reverberates not only into the future but into the past as well. It seemed clear before much work was done that no *definitive* statement could be made about Malamud's first work until his last had been done.

For all of these reasons the scope of *Bernard Malamud* had to be modest. Its primary aim is to supply the reader with as clear and yet as restrained an approach as possible to the fiction. By and large, the organization of the work reflects this aim. The texts used are almost exclusively the novels and collected short stories, and they are considered in that order.

A second aim, however, is also implicit in the organization. From these materials an attempt has been made to construct a pattern of development which illuminates the author's intent and at the same time supplies a basis for gauging his development and evaluating his achievement to date. No doubt, even this appears a too-ambitious project in dealing with a writer who has published only three novels and two volumes of short stories; and so it would be were it not that Malamud's fiction has apparently taken a clearly definable shape. His career represents, in fact, a remarkable literary progress in which he has sought, through the resources of diverse novelistic modes, to give wider and more dramatic impact to his central themes. And it is this development, symmetrical beyond my early hopes, which has allowed me to undertake this study with a sense of completion. It has supplied the unifying thread in my interpretation of the novels, and it has dictated the organization and the treatment of the short stories. Ultimately, it has served as the basis for my critical evaluation of both the novels and the stories.

With one exception, I have avoided all but occasional biographical or historical references. The exception is the short first chapter, "The Minority Writer as Majority," which was prompted as much by my reading of criticism as by anything within the primary texts. Two of Malamud's novels and nearly all his short stories are centrally concerned with Jewish issues; and, while such an interest might have been a passport to oblivion twenty years ago, it is hard to determine today if the author's great popularity is the result of his artistry or of his subject matter. However it has come about, those Jewish writers who, like Malamud, cultivate their Jewishness as subject matter are currently among our most respected writers. It seemed necessary, therefore, to say something about this issue if only to mitigate some of the confusions it has engendered and which obscure a clear understanding of Malamud's fiction. My job was not to discover what Malamud can tell us of the cultural movement, but what the movement might tell us of Malamud—a writer who shares many of the preoccupations of his fellow Jewish authors but who is to be distinguished from them by his special interests and intents. The opportunity to do this, moreover, also supplied the means of placing Malamud in the wider context of contemporary culture.

A good deal of whatever success I have had in this undertaking is directly due to the kindness and the wisdom of many friends, and I would like to acknowledge that debt. In particular, my gratitude goes to Professors Marvin Singleton and John Palmer, and to Paul Love, Douglas Scott, and Thomas Sturak, who have either read and criticized portions of the manuscript or have encouraged me in the writing of it. I want also to thank Bernard Malamud for his kindness in answering my numerous queries. My greatest debt, however, is to my wife, Estelle, for her patience and thoughtfulness.

For permission to quote from the ensuing works, I am indebted to Bernard Malamud and to Farrar, Straus and Company, Inc., publishers of *The Assistant, The Magic Barrel, A New Life,* and *Idiots First.*

SIDNEY RICHMAN

California State College at Los Angeles

Contents

Chronology

1914 Bernard Malamud born in Brooklyn, New York. Parents: Bertha and Max Malamud.

1928- Student at Erasmus Hall High School.
1932

1932- Student at City College of New York. Awarded Bache-
1936 lor's degree in 1934.

1937- Student at Columbia University. Awarded Master's de-
1938 gree in 1942.

1940 Worked as clerk in Bureau of Census, Washington, D.C.

1940- Taught evening classes at Erasmus Hall High School.
1948

1941 Began writing short stories.

1945 Married Ann de Chiara; lived in Greenwich Village.

1947 Birth of son Paul.

1948- Taught evening classes at Harlem Evening High School.
1949

1949- Member of the faculty of Oregon State College, Cor-
1961 vallis, Oregon.

1950 Stories appear in *Harper's Bazaar, Partisan Review, Commentary.*

1952 *The Natural.* Birth of daughter Janna.

1956 Spent in Rome and traveling in Europe.

1957 *The Assistant.*

1958 *The Magic Barrel.*

1959 Received National Book Award for *The Magic Barrel.*

1961 *A New Life.* Joined the faculty of Bennington College, Bennington, Vermont.

1963 *Idiots First.* Travel in England and Italy.

1965 Travel in Soviet Union, France, and Spain.

Bernard Malamud

CHAPTER *1*

The Minority Writer as Majority

"The Jews are absolutely the very *stuff* of drama."[1]
BERNARD MALAMUD

THE HIGHLY RESPECTED Catholic laymen's journal, *Ramparts*, recently devoted an issue to a symposium on the modern American Jew and, in particular, on the modern American Jewish writer. Lest the conjunction appear odd, Leslie Fiedler, who is both a contributor and an editor, indirectly clarified everything. "We live," he wrote, "at a moment when everywhere in the realm of prose Jewish writers have discovered their Jewishness to be an eminently marketable commodity, their much vaunted alienation to be their passport into the heart of Gentile American culture." And with a curious mixture of aggressive satire and candor, Fiedler presents evidence of the impact upon American society of Jewish attitudes, preoccupations, and even appetites, not only in literature but in almost everything else—from supermarket food displays to university faculties.[2]

That Fiedler is substantially correct in his contentions about modern Jewish writers is persuasive—not only from the cogency of his portrait but from the fact that it can be duplicated and reduplicated in a dozen other journals which of late have debated something called the "Jewish problem." And, if the mere number of articles suddenly devoted to the subject will not suffice, then a glance at the best-seller lists should certainly confirm his argument. For the first time in American literary history, the "Jewish writer" has, as Fiedler indicates, used his very Jewishness to effect an imaginative entry into American literature; and he has done so on a large and a remarkably varied front. Where writers like Saul Bellow and Bernard

Malamud and Philip Roth, among the chief novelists of our day, have found signal inspiration in the life of the American Jew, there are large numbers of others like Harvey Swados and Norman Mailer, J. D. Salinger and Herbert Gold who have on occasion revealed that the Jew is a peculiarly dramatic symbol for man's struggle in the modern world. Moreover, to judge by the recent critical success of such books as Norman Fruchter's *Coat Upon a Stick* or Bruce Friedman's *Stern,* the humanization of the Jew continues unabated, testifying to the perceptiveness of Ihab Hassan's comment "that the urban Jewish writer, like the Southern novelist, has emerged from the tragic underground of culture as a true spokesman of mid-century America."[3]

Needless to say, such a development, which is as sudden as it is unusual, is only indirectly an artistic issue. As Fiedler and most commentators on the subject have shown, the sudden prominence of Jewish themes in literature reflects some remarkable adjustments in our entire culture; and as such it attracts explanations at the same time that it confounds them. So exaggerated have been the claims, and so diverse the explanations, that it has become quite clear that if the cardinal novelty of present-day literature is the ascendancy of the minority writer and the refashioning of the Jew into a malleable and a persuasive symbol of Everyman, then it is the cardinal confusion of present-day literature as well. Indeed, the serious Jewish writer is today caught in the curious situation which finds the very ferment of comment increasing sales at the same time it is increasing misunderstandings. If Philip Roth's award-winning stories about the agonies of suburban Jews in *Goodbye, Columbus* tell us, as they do, a good deal about the underground needs of men everywhere, then the charges of anti-Semitism which greeted the author tell us also of the underground guilt which is certainly as crucial an aspect of the celebration of things Jewish as is the weighty problem of urban experience or the even weightier problem of identity. In any case, one must wonder if the charges against Roth have any validity in an interpretation of his work; and one must also wonder if the praise of the book is a testament to its literary merit or its subject matter. Assuredly the enthusiasm which has greeted, and in part created, a movement that counts among its members such figures as Herman Wouk and Leon Uris, as well as Bellow and Roth and Malamud, can just as easily threaten judgment as support it.

I *The "Jewishness" of Malamud*

But perhaps nothing so clearly indicates the hazards posed for criticism by this psycho-cultural movement than this opening chapter to a study of Bernard Malamud's fiction. At the moment Malamud is generally considered one of our most important contemporary writers, and his reputation is not only enormous but international. Whether or not he desires it, he has on the basis of a career hardly a decade old been charged with the task not only of shaping present literature but of supplying the basis for a future one. Faced with acclaim of this order, a critic could wish nothing more than to begin at the beginning, with the fiction itself. But the nature of Malamud's popularity makes this impossible. In any survey of the contemporary literary or cultural scene his name is so prominently featured, and for such a variety of reasons, that the critic despairs of finding the actual grounds of his appeal. The hub of the problem is precisely his "Jewishness." In reading some of Malamud's critics, one suspects that it is less his art than his subject which is the center of interest. Too often there is the uneasy sensation that the subject is not really a writer who happens also to be a Jew but a Jew who happens also to be a writer. In any case, one must in part rescue Malamud from many of the conditions of his fame; and one is obliged to do so at the point where his particularly literary concerns carry over into wider and more ambiguous social concerns.

To isolate the "real" Malamud with any precision, however, carries its own dangers. In retreat from the "accidents" of history, one tends to deny history altogether, to rest content with some variation of Malamud's own statement that he writes of Jewish materials "because I know it."[4] But, if such statements are refreshingly straightforward, they tend to impoverish a perfectly reasonable interpretative approach which only the excessiveness of sociological criticism has called into doubt. The fact that Malamud writes of Jews is at best only interesting; but the fact that his imaginative understanding of

Jewish issues is shared by a host of fellow writers, and that together they have struck a deep reaction in the contemporary consciousness, argues that "history" *is* implicated in Malamud's Jewish materials. Indeed, the fact that an entire generation of Jewish-American writers has managed in the space of ten or fifteen years to lose the status of "special cases" and create for themselves a central place in American culture argues for Isaac Rosenfeld's old claim "that whatever contributions Jewish writers may make to American literature will depend on matters beyond their control as writers."[5]

Rosenfeld was correct; but if one asks after the nature of these "matters," he is immediately troubled by a striking irony. For the sudden emergence of the Jewish-American author has occurred at precisely the moment when few if any special conditions need bother him. Racial amity is no longer the myth which so many Jewish writers yearned for in the past. Having won his long struggle for a place in society, the Jew is as free as any man to write as an American and not as a minority figure. But perplexingly, one finds that the best of Malamud's novels, and the best of his stories, willfully culti-vate attitudes and backgrounds which are as specifically Jewish as the author can make them and which often represent a return to conditions long past. Moreover, these are exactly the works which have received the largest share of critical and popular acclaim.

Nor is Malamud alone in this. If only to a lesser extent, the same phenomenon is present in the fiction of many of his con-temporaries; and surely it is present in the enthusiasm which has greeted the stories and novels of such writers as Singer and Babel. Not only has the Jewish writer come into prominence when he has seemingly disappeared as a separate entity, but both the theme and the trappings of his former alienation have become the indispensable features of that prominence.

The irony is compounded when one recalls that, in the past, alienation was the single most important ingredient in denying the Jew an essential voice in his adopted country. Aside from the few genuine attempts to capture the truth of Jewish experience in America—Abraham Cahan and Henry Roth come quickly to mind (and both have only recently been reprinted)—the history of Jewish-American literature to recent times resembles a disturbingly fictive tour through an America as unreal as love or hostility might make it. The greatness of any writer is perhaps identifiable by what he does not let himself or his readers forget about human existence; but the burden of the Jewish writer has always been one of deliberate forgetfulness. Faced with the possibility of an end to the torments of alienation which America presented, the Jewish writer has in the main devoted himself to forwarding that possibility.

And the primary resource open to him was a literature of adaptation, a willful counterfeiting of his own and his people's identity. It is not too much to say, in fact, that literature as public relations has been for almost a century the standard mode of expression among Jewish-American writers. That their efforts met with success is also undeniable, for it lives on in the multitude of identities through which the Jew was turned into a neat, conformable American: the endless stream of wise bumblers, pious bookstore owners, gentle savants, and garrulous but loving mothers who, while pleasant, are no more interesting, humanly speaking, than the long-haired radicals or aggressive moneylenders who fill the pages of anti-Semitic literature and who indeed called them into existence. Simply, the Jewish writer who would give human as opposed to what Rosenfeld called "sociological acknowledgment"[6] to his people was rare in the past. Not so curiously, the Jewish writer who would do so was even rarer than the Gentile. It is therefore not in the least remarkable that, as Fiedler has written, the novel in which Jewish writers dealt with their experiences in America not only falls "short of final excellence, but . . . remains somehow irrelevant to the main lines of development of fiction in the United States."[7]

II *The Self Alone*

That Fiedler's contention no longer applies indicates some powerful changes in recent Jewish history; and, to judge by the works of such writers as Roth and Malamud, the principal one is the feeling that the contemporary Jew is not only the beneficiary of a remarkably successful assimilative drive but also the victim of it. A predominant belief in modern Jewish prose, but particularly in the prose of Malamud, is that when man strives to accommodate himself to the world at the expense of self, the measure of his success is often times indistinguishable from his failure; that frequently what is attained is only what the Jews in Roth's stories attain: a suburban make-believe where glutted freezers give surrogate consolation to hungers that are insatiable and where the vaunted "good life" is more often than not a system of blinders to screen men from the hollowness within and the catastrophic possibilities without.

If the rise of minority literature signifies anything clearly, it is that the Jewish novelist has finished with the job of adjusting to his culture and can now, in Lionel Trilling's words, devote himself to the truth that "In its essence literature is concerned with self, and the particular concern of the literature of the past two centuries has been with the self in its standing quarrel with culture."⁸ The contemporary form of that quarrel has been bequeathed to the American Jew by virtue of his history. In having effected an end to social alienation, he has reaped a more profound, if not so threatening, alienation as any he knew in the past. If not cut off from society, he is cut off from himself. And this theme permeates Malamud's fiction. His essential hero is the unintegrated mask-wearer seeking for a connection with the world. But in failing to attain connection with his own nature, he finds that the world to which he fits his face turns into a chaos of unfulfillment. Perhaps the most important fact of Malamud's characterizations is that his Jews *do* possess an ancient identity and that they bear it, consciously or unconsciously, through a hall of historical mirrors. And their relationship to this identity determines their development.

Primarily, it is the struggle to establish unity with some unacknowledged center of one's personality, a quest for lost roots, which directs Malamud's Jewish heroes. Where once in Jewish-American literature the mother was celebrated for her support of the assimilative task, Malamud's characters must regain the way of the father, the carrier of ancient traditions. The difficulties of the task, and the stern restrictions Malamud places on success, will be investigated in later chapters. Ultimately, however, the "way" his heroes are obliged to take simply reverses the traditional success story which the Jew had to accept as his motivating dream in America. The Morris

Bobers and the S. Levins in Malamud's fictional world succeed as men only by virtue of their failures in society. Were it not that their suffering deflects them from their own achievements, they might well intone: What profits it a man if he gains the world and loses himself?

What sustains these heroes is Malamud's belief, to paraphrase Frankie Alpine in *The Assistant,* that man is better than he is; that there is a zone of goodness, a conscience, bequeathed from the humane traditions of the past which can be proof against the present. It is this belief which was the subject of Malamud's acceptance speech on the occasion of receiving the National Book Award for *The Magic Barrel.* He said at that time: "I am quite tired of the colossally deceitful devaluation of man in this day. . . . Whatever the reason, his fall from grace in his eyes is betrayed by the words he has invented to describe himself as he is now: fragmented, abbreviated, other-directed, organizational. . . . The devaluation exists because he accepts it without protest."[9]

III *Struggle for Roots*

Needless to say, there is nothing particularly novel at the moment in the belief that the fall from grace can be arrested only by a seizure of the self, a struggle for roots within. That the Jewish writer can take as his special province the recoil of self from the exigencies of the affluent society, from the dreams of political and economic amelioration, only establishes his kinship with his fellow writers. As Ihab Hassan put it, the self is in recoil in all modern literature;[10] and the marginal man or the underground man, the picaresque saint or the *shlemihl,* are all symptoms of the same dilemma. The failure of philosophy to deliver truth; of politics, contentment; of economics, happiness—indeed the failure of man to deliver man is at best only cliché; and so the Jew has no priority as marginal man—at least he no longer has. Perhaps the most that can be said of the Jewish writer's eloquence is that, by virtue of his own history and the history of his literature in this country, he is more sensitive to the texture of the present than most. What might have been in the past a problem peculiar to Jews is today mankind's problem. Perhaps Franz Kafka's gnomic summation of his own relationship to his people, an answer which curiously contains both denial and ironic acquiesence, is the best revelation of this fact: "What have I in common with Jews? I have hardly anything in common with myself."[11]

Like many of his fellow Jewish-American writers, Malamud speaks for those who "have hardly anything in common" with themselves and who are seeking, through a maze of social and philosophical blind-alleys, for a reattainment of self. As Malamud points out again and again in his fiction, Jewishness is not a necessary ingredient in this success. In *The Natural,* his first novel, there are no Jewish characters; and yet the myth of salvation which dominates his fiction generally is more clearly indicated in it than in any of his later novels. At most, Malamud's Jews are simply symbols for all men who suffer to be better than they are or whose personalities are riven by what Bellow once termed the debate between the real and the pretender soul.

But while Malamud goes far to make this point (so far, in fact, that he refuses to distinguish Jewish ethics from Christian or Humanistic ethics), it is nonetheless true that it is *only* his Jews or, in the case of Frankie Alpine, the Gentile who becomes a Jew, who ultimately succeed in his fiction. The Gentile may chart the way, as Roy Hobbes of *The Natural* does; but he cannot attain the goal. That is to say, if the author's intent is to generalize the Jew into a construct representing all men, it is the redemptive forces implicit in his dramatic portrait of Jews which finally persuades the reader that men can be better than they are.

IV *Literary Tradition*

That Malamud can so move his reader is the result of a number of literary strategies. Persuasion lies in part in the ambiguities of his affirmation and in part in the resources of a remarkably flexible style. But most importantly, Malamud convinces because he has regained in his finest work the tragic vision which has been central to Jewish expression for ages. While it would be foolish to try to place an author so receptive to the currents of fictional technique in any single tradition, there are sufficient grounds to believe that in some ways, and perhaps intuitively, Malamud does belong in the tradition of East European

Yiddish storytelling; for to support his conception of Morris Bober the grocer, or Leo Finkle the Yeshivah student, he has evoked a world in which both the settings and the distinctive tensions are highly reminiscent of the "literature of the Pale," and particularly the tales of such writers as Sholom Aleichem and I. L. Peretz.

In the pages of *The Assistant* and many of the stories in *The Magic Barrel*, a kind of timeless New York ghetto stands guard against all attempts at assimilation; and it is in most particulars only another instance of the Pale: that now lost world of small villages or *shtetls* in Eastern Europe where the Jews, forced by law to abide in daily insecurity and denied access to the larger world, managed to maintain and develop a cultural and communal tradition based upon adherence to Talmudic principles and tested in a crucible that demanded both the tragic vision and the tragic affirmation which has sustained Jewish expression since the days of Job. In most of Malamud's stories the Pale remains as a spiritual topography which defines the characters' insecurity and dread at the same time that it becomes the basis for their potential reinstatement in grace. As Marcus Klein put it, Malamud's fiction has "depended upon the *shtetl* problem and the *shtetl* sense . . . of permanent precariousness, of proximity with the mythical past."[12] In Malamud's world, alienation from modern history, needs unsatisfied, and hopes blasted are what recall the characters to what is best in them; and his distinctive settings—dark and disconsolate rooms, barred doors, groceries in cellars—are the tangible signs of their alienation.

But perhaps the best description of Malamud's settings was not written of Malamud's but of Sholom Aleichem's world, and can be found in Isaac Rosenfeld's portrait of the village of Kasrilevke, the setting where the "Bard of the Pale" founded his stories. It was a village, Rosenfeld wrote, which "was guarded but exhausted by an old religion which had never learned to rationalize adaptation to the world." Within it, he added, Aleichem constructed

> . . . a comedy of endurance, balancing the fantastic excess of misfortune . . . against the precious but useless resources of the human spirit which . . . can even overwhelm the world with enthusiasm, and yet remains no less impotent than the despair

it sedulously avoids. In this respect, Sholom Aleichem was in the great tradition of Chassidism, to which he provided the secular counterpart. Enthusiasm and ecstasy are the ideal limits of his humor, just as they were the final values of the Chassid's worship.[13]

Enthusiasm and ecstasy are frequently also the ideal limits of Malamud's humor, as they are of Bellow's humor. Their characters' triumphs often seem indistinguishable from their impotent tears or their unheard whoops of joy. But Malamud's uses of *Chassidism* will be considered later. More to the point is his affinity to the theme of redemptive suffering and to the comic mode by which he supports that theme. "The world envies us," one of Aleichem's principal characters has said, "because we suffer." Caught in a similarly resonant masochism, Malamud's Jews might say the same thing—and at times do. Throughout his fiction, the theme of victory through defeat is constant; for it is only when his needs remain unsatisfied that Malamud's hero can recognize the form of his most human needs. In the best of his stories and in his best novel, Malamud has re-created the same disconsolate and hungry world one finds in the masters of nineteenth-century Yiddish folk realism; and, like them, but with his own unique powers, he has filled it also with spiritual illuminations. Indeed, his underground world must seem to the author the only possible condition for becoming a man.

V *Malamud's Comic Mode*

Malamud's instinctive affinity to both the themes and the special concerns of East European Jewish literature is clearest in his comedy. If refracted by time and place, it is on the whole the same kind of comedy, "the comedy of exile," which pervades the work of Sholom Aleichem. "The one offense which comedy cannot endure," it has been written, "is that a man should forget he is a man." As we will see, laughter becomes in Malamud's writing and even, as in *The Assistant,* his most terrifying writing, the prime agency in exposing a man to his own manhood. Necessarily it also becomes, as it was with Aleichem, the only form of affirmation, a grotesque and offbeat laugh in the face of reality.

It is perhaps unnecessary to add that comedy is probably the prevailing mode in most of our serious literature today, and often enough it is the same kind of comedy that has represented the Jews' primary mode of spiritual accommodation to the inhumanity of the world. In truth, nothing so cogently expresses the universality of the Jewish experience than the fact that the Jewish comedian, though he has proliferated wildly of late, no longer has any priority as comedian. Those "holy" jokes which served to remind the Jew of his true identity now serve such writers as Ralph Ellison in *The Invisible Man* and such "stand-up" comics as Dick Gregory. In these men, as in Malamud, laughter is the vehicle for stripping away the masks by which man forgets he is a man.

But in saying so much, of course, one remembers the comedy of Aristophanes and realizes that it is misleading to pursue the theme of Jewishness too far. That the serious Jewish-American novelist can investigate his special experiences and yet speak so tellingly means only that his concerns and his readers have at last come together. There are times, Herman Hesse somewhere remarks, when whole generations are out of touch with their present and their past and so lose the power to understand themselves. This has been the agony of successive generations of Jews; but if one is attentive to the intent and the meaning of present-day literature, whether the work of Gentile or Jew, he recognizes that this is such a time for all men. Moreover, in an age teetering on total annihilation, when little direction can be derived from our most cherished modern dreams, the Jew's old message that we all live on the Pale, threatened by extinction from within and without, and his belief that we can survive only by recourse to what is best in us, must strike deeply into all responsive men who revere their separate heritages and who long to be better than the world will seemingly permit them to be.

In this, again, Malamud offers convincing testimony. In his first novel there are no Jews. But, as with all his later works, the message of *The Natural* is clear: It is only by the act of succumbing to the good within, by renouncing the demands of the world, that man may find the way to re-attain the world.

CHAPTER 2

The Natural

> "The values and distinctions that in normal life
> seem important disappear with the terrifying as-
> similation of the self into what formerly was
> only otherness."[1]
>
> JOSEPH CAMPBELL

BERNARD MALAMUD'S first novel, *The Natural,* remains to this day the most ambiguous of his works and the most unrepresentative. To many, the book seems to be either a false start or an exercise in mythic madness; and even so recent a survey of Malamud's fiction as Granville Hicks's essay in *The Creative Present* (1963) considers the novel with the preliminary note that "I am not sure what to make of the book as a whole," and then proceeds to treat it as irrelevant to Malamud's later career.[2]

For this bewilderment and this dismissal of the book, Mr. Hicks is to be pardoned. *The Natural* is one of the most baffling novels of the 1950's, and it is doubly so when one attempts to see it as the work of a descendant of "the great realistic masters of Yiddish literature."[3] Said to be inspired by an Arthur Daley column in the *New York Times,*[4] the book traces the rise and fall of a phenomenally gifted baseball player from his teens to his mid-thirties; and nowhere is there a Jew or a mention of one. And as if a novel about baseball were not sufficiently odd, the author persists in skirting such a bizarre path between humor and symbol, myth and burlesque, that at times it is impossible to distinguish the real intent. Narrated in a voice composed of equal parts Mel Allen and James Joyce, the history of Roy Hobbes's attempts to win fame and fortune as a big-league ball-player is fused together out of scraps of Homer's Troy, Malory's

Britain, and Ring Lardner's New York. With a cursory reading the reader must suspect that it is all a hoax or at the least that Malamud's career is remarkably discontinuous.

I *Theme and Technique*

But such reactions, if pardonable, are not true. If the major difficulty in placing *The Natural* in proper perspective was heretofore its obvious contrast to the author's second novel, then the appearance of Malamud's third novel, as well as his two volumes of short stories, obviates a good deal of the difficulty. Considered in the light of this later work, *The Natural* belongs to a pattern of development which has been curiously consistent from first to last. Though the half-rube, half-knightly Roy Hobbes of *The Natural* gives way in *The Assistant* to a Jewish grocer and his helper, and though both of these are superseded in Malamud's last novel by a Jewish college instructor, all three are drawn together by the form of their struggles and by the nature of their limitations. *The Natural* is a book about baseball; but it is also about the ritual trial which, as Ihab Hassan said of *The Assistant* but might as easily have said of *A New Life*, "transforms a man into a mensch."[5]

If *The Natural* differs markedly from the author's later works, therefore, the difference is primarily a question of literary manner, of a grail or romance conversion rather than an Essene conversion. In itself, the fact illuminates Malamud's contention that the way to redemption has no priority as the way of the Jews.[6] At the same time it suggests what is perhaps most interesting about Malamud's fiction, which is not alone his attempt to vitalize an ancient theme of redemption in an age that thrives on despair and denigration, but rather his effort to discover a style and form which can most persuasively embody the theme. *The Natural* introduces Malamud in his first extensive struggle with technique. Out of the book, its failures even more than its successes, emerge the materials of his later novels. Out of all three emerge the image of a writer in our day rare in the extreme—an experimental artist for whom each successive work, no matter the recurrent unity of theme, represents a fresh opportunity for the creation of a new mode of persuasiveness.

The unity of Malamud's themes is our first concern, however;

and in this also *The Natural* is most illuminating. In shaping the action of the work in terms of the language of myth, Malamud has supplied the reader with an outline of his moral imperatives which is clearer than in any of his later works. Formally, *The Natural* is divided into two sections. The first deals with the adventures, triumphs, and defeat of the nineteen-year-old Hobbes who, armed only with Wonderboy, the bat he has hewn from a lightning-blasted oak tree and which serves throughout as the symbol of his potential for rebirth, is entrained to Chicago for a tryout as pitcher with the Cubs; the second picks up the narrative years later when a coarser if not maturer Roy, still bearing Wonderboy, returns to the big-league intent on a new start. Though uneven in size, the events of the first part of *The Natural* clearly parallel the events of the second; and, taken together, they recapitulate the mythic formula of Initiation, Separation, and Return. But most importantly, the repetition serves to dramatize the author's belief that the way to redemption lies in part in the hero's reactions to his own past and his ability to understand it, thereby escaping its inherent limitations. Roy's inability to do so is the basis of his failure. The experiences of part one, only a fifth of the narrative, lead Roy only into similar though expanded misfortunes in part two, and so into failure. As the ballplayer tells himself on the final page, "I never did learn anything out of my past life, now I have to suffer again."[7]

In both sections, moreover, Roy Hobbes follows a mythic direction, for he is "Easterning," as will Frankie Alpine of *The Assistant,* toward a destiny he both fears and desires but, in any case, only half understands. He is as indeterminate in his identity as is the speed-confused landscape he observes from the rushing train window. One of his first gestures in the novel is to strike a match and gaze from the window. But the glass becomes a mirror, a favorite image in Malamud's fiction, which gives back to the player an ambiguous reflection. On the one hand, Roy's reflection suggests a symbol of enslavement, his face obscuring the passing world—a tortured landscape of twisted trees. Curiously, however, the image also suggests liberty.

This odd fusion of possibility and enslavement is also implicated in Roy's history, about which the reader is never told much. In the fashion of the young Lochinvar, he has materialized

out of a mysterious West that resolves itself into a series of
primitive images and veiled allusions. But Roy's past is clearly
the "past" of all Malamud's major characters: a dark world il-
luminated by a few curative recollections which collide with the
dark and chart the hero's quandary. Like Frankie Alpine who
bears with him the image of St. Francis and snow, an image
wrenched out of a gloomy and suffering world, or like S. Levin,
who carries the precious reminder of the sun striking the soles
of his shoes in a flea-bitten basement, Roy Hobbes has memories
which are fixed in 'the disparate recollections of a young boy in
a green world—a primordial image of the young God that is
talisman against other memories: a father who had taught him
to play ball, but who had been driven to drink and despair by
a mother who "didn't love anybody" (186).

The colliding images of the past and the overtones of incest
and patriarchal destruction are the frame and the index to the
mature problem. All the temptresses in the novel bear with them
the stigmata of the false mother, and all of Roy's guides and
mentors serve as symbols of the wounded father who can be
reclaimed only by the hero's successful refusal to succumb to
the mother. Moreover, the two sets of images are, like the yolk
and the white of a single egg, contained within Roy's own personality as his ontological dilemma and supply both his motivation and the trailing fantasies which beset him throughout the
novel. In his sleeper on a train, Roy exalts in his call to destiny
at the same time that he fears it—for in the tradition of all grail
heroes, before he can attain transcendence he must, in effect,
submit to a transformation that slays the "lower" self. Or, as
Jonathan Baumbach has suggested, "before Roy can emerge as
King, he must battle past the limitations of bumpkin (Hobbes)
within."[8]

II *Roy Hobbes*

As in most forms of the grail-myth, the young knight has his
initiatory guide who functions in the capacity of the stricken
father. In the first section of the novel it is the drunken scout
and one-time catcher, Sam Simpson, who sees in Roy the promise of his own salvation and who arranges Roy's first knightly
joust. On board the train is Walter (the Whammer) Whambold,
the leading batter of the American League, who serenely agrees

to Sam's challenge that he face Roy's pitches when the train is mysteriously halted. The duel, held beside the tracks, becomes a grotesquely meaningful confrontation, for batter and pitcher hold out to one another the form of their own fears. To the untested Roy, the Whammer assumes the shape of his own earthly and unknightly limitations, "gigantic. . . . with the wood held like a caveman's ax on his shoulder." To the suddenly apprehensive Whammer, the young pitcher has all the features of a youthful undertaker sent to exact punishment for the batter's own limitations. The meeting serves as a clear prefiguring of the final battle in the book; then a much older Roy must face a young pitcher and so rescue himself or, for his unworthiness and lack of humility, fall before the inevitable sequence of natural determinism—as, indeed, Walter the Whammer falls, the victim of three peerless lyrical strikes, each "like a white pigeon." At thirty-three the Whammer emerges from his duel with the opposing self "an old man," without promise of resurrection (28-30).

Roy's glory, however, is shadowed by two gloomy developments. His final pitch has struck Sam Simpson's scarecrow chest and, in a matter of hours, precipitates his death and raises the ambiguous problem of Roy's responsibility. But even more importantly, his triumph over the Whammer brings the young player to the attention of Harriet Bird, the "silver-eyed mermaid," who seems a strangely probable mixture of castrating woman and Morgan le Fay, but who in reality, or at least in the tradition of grail literature, has been sent to test the hero's worthiness and exact punishment when he fails (16). Nor is Roy the only one. Harriet turns out to be the unknown woman who has mysteriously slain two other athletes with silver bullets when, presumably, they had been unable to answer the series of questions which Harriet now puts to Roy concerning the nature of his quest. And the questions are all-important. As Jessie Weston suggests in her study of the grail cycle, "From the records of his partial success we gather that he [the hero] ought to have enquired concerning the nature of the Grail, and that this enquiry would have resulted in the restoration to fruitfulness of a Waste Land. . . ."[9] However, when Harriet asks Roy why he wants to become a big-league player, he, forgetful of his father and the now dead scout, can only reply in terms of unflattering selfishness: To be the "best there ever was in the game" (33).

[32]

In the final pages of the first section, Harriet questions Roy again. In her room in a Chicago hotel—"an enormous four-section fortress"—Harriet, with a pistol in her hand, asks: "Roy, will you be the best there ever was in the game?" When he replies affirmatively, Harriet discharges a silver bullet which Roy, a natural player, "sought with his bare hands to catch . . . but it eluded him, and to his horror, bounced into his gut" (40-41).

Part Two picks up the narrative after an interval of several years and records Roy Hobbes's efforts to create a new life. Now thirty-four, he assumes a position as outfielder with the National League's last place New York Knights, a team so disorganized that even the ministrations of a professional hypnotist fail to help it. The team's greatest asset, the practical joker Bump Bailey, is, like the Whammer, more gorilla than hero; he spends most of his time inventing means to bedevil his teammates. But, most particularly, Bump's failure as a hero is most evident in his offhand treatment of the team's manager (and "Father"), Pop Fisher, a woebegone figure of the injured king who, with athlete's foot on his hands, dances his dismay on the sun-parched summer field and despairs of ever attaining his greatest ambition, the winning of the pennant.

The events of the latter part of the novel follow with some consistency, though farcical consistency, the pattern of the grail-quest, including a trip to a netherworld nightclub, the Pot of Fire, where Roy overcomes magic with magic. Against the forces of "darkness," in particular the co-owner of the team, the tower-dwelling Judge Goodwill Banner, Roy attempts to salvage his life. His main antagonists are a confused whirl of spectral figures; but chief among them is the Mephistophelian Gus Sands, "King of the Bookies," and the red-haired temptress Memo Paris, who is both Bump Bailey's girl friend and Pop Fisher's niece. At the beginning of the section Roy, by virtue of Bump's joke, has had Memo in bed; and his pursuit of her through the remainder of the novel becomes a false grail pursuit, a struggle for un-retainable ecstasy.

But at the same time, the second part of the book is devoted in large part to the record of Roy's heroics on the field. Sustained by his still matchless physical prowess—the emblem of his continuing potential for true heroism—the player wins through to a glowing if partial success. Despite his age, his playing is breathtaking. The first time at bat he *does* sock the cover off the ball and so begins the reclamation of the wasteland: "Wonderboy flashed in the sun. It caught the sphere where it was biggest. A noise like a twenty-one gun salute cracked the sky. There was a straining, ripping sound and a few drops of rain spattered to the ground" (80). And the hit is only one of several. In a matter of weeks, baseball fans are aware of a phenomenal new presence. With Wonderboy at his shoulder, Roy struggles out of anonymity and out of the limitations of his age and with bewildering rapidity breaks almost every record for a "rookie" player. In his wake the Knights are magically cured of their clumsiness; Bump Bailey is killed by crashing into an outfield wall in a frustrated attempt to outdo Roy; and Pop Fisher, cheering and crying from the sidelines, is restored to ebullient health.

But if Roy is a peerless player, he is by no means a perfect one. With success, his ego swells enormously, blinding him both to his responsibility to Pop Fisher and to the team. Unable to submerge his appetite to the refinement of spiritual needs, he persists in transferring a transcendental quest into an all too earthly quest for Memo Paris, who like Harriet Bird, bears all the stigmata of the enchantress—in particular the flaming orange hair that Malamud, in the fashion of Balzac, delights in ascribing to his Satanic anti-heroes. But Memo, unlike the briefly sketched Harriet, is also characterized by distinctively human corruptions—the mark of which, as it will be for the female instructor in *A New Life*, is a fibroma of the breast. Motivated by a deep and abiding desire to avoid serious human commitment, Memo loathes Roy both for his prowess and for his responsibility in the death of her bird-minded and loveless lover, Bump Bailey —a responsibility which Roy, to his shame, can no more consciously acknowledge than he can his responsibility for the demise of Sam Simpson. Allying herself with Gus Sands and Judge Goodwill Banner, who stand to gain large sums of money if the Knights lose the pennant, Memo manipulates Roy's hunger beyond endurance with an odd blend of feminine blandishments and Medea-like magic.

But Roy's chief adversary only wears the form of Memo Paris. All his problems continue to be rooted in a corruption of the Ego. Despite his dream of transcendence, he is still too much the Whammer and Bump—"the kind of gorilla he had more than once fought half to death for no reason he could think of" —to recognize the nature of his calling (52). Symptomatically, he constantly retreats in fear from a confrontation either with self or with the suffering he experiences for his lapses. And matching his insatiable greed for Memo and for success, which he still sees as the state of being "the best there ever was in the game," Roy's efforts to hide the guilt he feels for his past and present failures become progressively more desperate. Unlike the grail knight who bore the evidence of his perfidy for all to see in a gesture of humility, Roy hides the secrets of his past from all eyes.

Only Roy's childhood remains as an image of uncorrupted heroism, and he longs for a return to that state with the despair of the unwilling knight yearning for unconscious innocence. Against the astonishing array of phantoms which his guilt breeds, he can only pose the memory of himself as a youngster when, with "a dog, a stick, an aloneness he loved," he had in the guise of the young vegetation God wandered through green forests (117). Ironically, however, it is precisely such memories which allow Roy to intuit his failings. Unconsciously, he knows the right path. From every encounter with Memo his playing suffers; and because of his inability to say "yes" to his role in the deaths of Sam Simpson or Bump Bailey, or to his responsibility to Pop Fisher, he not only suffers on the field but must encounter, like knights in the Chapel Perilous, the visitations of bats, monsters, and formless spectres.

Like many of Malamud's heroes, Roy is the image of the unintegrated man, the hero who acts incorrectly despite his awareness. From this lack of integration, his pain proceeds. Trapped between the way of spirit and flesh, natural man and hero, there is only wave after wave of agony. So Roy yearns, as will Frankie Alpine, for integration at any cost. Understandably he chooses the easier course; he decides for a state of "negative self-determinism" which will transform his desire for Memo and his egoistic struggle to be best into a passion sufficient to blot out the awareness of his surrender to the dark forces within. Symbolically, the desire is tantamount to the destruction of the child within. In mid-season, with the Knights figuring promi-

nently in the pennant race, the fans throw a "Roy Hobbes Day";
and in return they listen to his declaration (he had forgotten
that he had meant to "thank them for their favor and say what
a good team the Knights were and how he enjoyed working for
Pop Fisher"): "I will do my best—the best I am able—to be
the greatest there ever was in the game" (114). Afterwards, with
Memo driving the white Mercedes the fans had given him, Roy
sees the image of a young boy with dog materialize from the
forest which fronts a dark road. In the ensuing instant, a whirl
of illusion and reality, Memo strikes the boy and drives on.
When Roy insists that he had heard a groan, she replies immediately, "That was yourself" (123). In despair Roy returns
to a hotel room peopled now with ghosts and phantoms, the old
"burning pain in his gut" suddenly intolerable (128).

Immediately the miracle-player undergoes an appalling slump.
For the next several weeks he either goes hitless or manages at
most a few weak dribbling singles. In despair, Pop Fisher, don-
ning his bandages, watches red-eyed as the New York Knights
lose their cohesiveness and sink downward in the league stand-
ings. As the headlines proclaim Roy's failures, he himself, "gasp-
ing for air . . . waited for the bloody silver bullet" that would put
an end to the protracted dying (140).

It is at the very bottom of this dark period, however, that fate
presents Roy with the possibility of reclaiming himself once
more—and it arrives in two interdependent forms. The first occurs
when Roy enters Chicago Stadium for a night game and is accosted by a man who—shades of Yankee mythology—begs the
slumping player to save the life of his hospitalized and hero-
worshipping boy by hitting a homer. Somehow recognizing that
such an act will mean both a break through the alienating ego
and a rescue by surrogate of the child within, Roy vows to
succeed. The second opportunity, however, rises from the limitations of the first. For innocence is *never* enough in Malamud's
novels. Nor is it enough for the true knight. Before the hero can
become the king he must, as Joseph Campbell put it, undergo
a purgation of "infantile images."[10] At best, innocence is only
a beginning, as it is only a beginning for Roy in Chicago.
Despite his aching determination, Wonderboy persists in looking
like a "sagging baloney"; and it is only when a strange lady with
a white rose rises from the stands, dispelling fragrance and con-

fidence in equal measure, that Roy can finally connect and
send the ball sailing "through the light up into the dark, like a
white star seeking an old constellation" (147).

III   *Iris Lemon*

The fragrance-distilling lady, who will live on with much
humanizing in Malamud's other novels, is named Iris Lemon;
and with her *The Natural* finds its normative center. Moreover,
it is Iris who introduces to the novel the richest of all Malamud's
subjects: the uses and abuses of love which animate and direct
all his novels and almost all his stories. However, in *The Natural*
the mythic form of the subject dominates the treatment. From
the beginning, Iris Lemon is a clear if curious blend of cosmic
mother with overtones of Ariadne and Dostoevsky's Sophie. Iris
functions as the exemplar of human potential, the living actuality that one can win through from suffering to a larger
and more meaningful life. In many ways, in fact, Iris' life history
parallels Roy's. An unwed mother in her teens—the victim of an
unknown man who had "pounced like a tiger"—Iris had devoted
her youth to the care of her daughter, discovering, as she later
reveals in a letter to Roy, that "the tender feelings I had in my
heart for her made up for a lot I had suffered." And now, at
thirty-three, Iris has taken up her life again, or finds it resur-
rected, at the point where she had abandoned it years before
(210-11).

But if Iris' life represents a commentary to Roy's own blasted
history, and its transmutation into a larger and more human
status, she is also the mysterious healer who can salvage the
hero through a crucial test. Indeed, she is the mirror of indoctrination and the way of salvation; and her analysis of the
hero-as-hero is significant in this regard. Not long after her
appearance in the stands, Iris and Roy spend an evening together by the shore of Lake Michigan—an ironic parallel to
an evening spent with Memo by a stagnant pool. Roy for the
first time reveals his past (the dawn of love in many of Malamud's works is often accompanied by a willingness to confess)
and finds it less difficult to relate than he had thought. The confession is for Malamud as for Dostoevsky a standard ordeal in
the ritual of rebirth, and it reverberates hugely in Roy's con-

sciousness. To her questions regarding his goals—a direct echo of Harriet's—he mouths the old selfish clichés; but they no longer seem convincing. And with a surprised sense of its correctness, he listens to Iris' own analysis of the hero. "I hate to see a hero fail," she tells him. "There are so few of them." In explanation, she informs Roy that "without heroes we're all plain people and don't know how far we can go. . . . I don't think you can do anything for anyone without giving up something of your own."

The hero as an impersonal symbol of all men had never before occurred to Roy who, in addition to all else, hated his fans. But the statement, surprising as it is, is only prologue. To complete her analysis of the hero, Iris invokes for the ballplayer, whose days are spent in an endless round of escaping pain, the ancient theme of redemption through suffering—a theme which reappears in all of Malamud's later work: "We have two lives, Roy, the life we learn with and the life we live with after that. Suffering is what brings us toward happiness."

This final paradox Roy cannot quite accept. Desperate and perplexed, as well as half in love, he leaps into the water and seeks the slime of the bottom in a gesture of fierce baptism. Returning winded to the surface, he sees the form of the frantic Iris floating beyond his head in the emblem of the Grail, luminously gold and charged with love. Later, in the midst of lovemaking and feeling "never so relaxed in sex," Roy listens to Iris' final declaration: "I forgot to tell you I am a grandmother" (155-63).

IV *The Hero's Failure*

Iris Lemon as grandmother instead of golden girl is, of course, a form of the ancient hag whom the knight must marry in order to attain his goal. But she is perhaps the personification of a still more ancient archetype. As Joseph Campbell puts it, she is the woman whose couches are "beaches of golden sand," and who unites in one the "ever mother, ever virgin" who "encompasses the encompassing, nourishes the nourishing, and is the life of everything that lives." Within her is united the good and bad, the sweet and sour (and so her name). The hero who can accept her "without undue commotion but with the kindness and assurance she requires," not only discovers that he "is potentially the king, the incarnate god of her created world,"

but also that her beauty "is redeemed by the eyes of understanding."[11]

But Roy cannot accept her. In his eyes, in fact, Iris' beauty is
despoiled. Resisting love with the same intensity with which
S. Levin later resists Pauline Gilley in *A New Life*, Roy returns
to New York where he seeks to drown his guilt in animalism.
Unlike the knight who must fast interminably in preparation for
his transcendence, Roy borrows a page from Babe Ruth and
gluts the hunger for rebirth and the pangs of unwilling love by
eating. In a climactic scene in which he is led on by the con-
niving Memo, Roy swamps his guilt with such quantities of food
that he falls to the floor unconscious. As with Harriet Bird, he
is the victim of a shattered gut that, with an accompaniment of
locomotive sounds, "flushed . . . him under" (191). While con-
valescing in the hospital, Roy encounters and succumbs to his
final temptations. Persuaded by Memo and Judge Banner, the
player denies categorically the lesson of his past and his own
conscience and agrees to throw the pennant-deciding game of
the season with the Pirates. True to his word, he takes to the
field and consumes the bitter pill of his wretchedness, while the
judge and Memo nod approbation from the tower; and Pop
Fisher, who "it seemed to Roy he had known all his life long,"
dodders graveward on a sideline bench (222).

The game, as improbable as a little-leaguer's nightmare, is
endlessly prolonged. Through inning after inning Roy limps
about in forlorn mimicry of determination, struggling against the
tag-ends of heroism which persist in bubbling sporadically to the
surface. Late in the game, however, they crowd into his wintering
frame like spring nettles; and for a moment failure and success
fuse in perilous balance. But the end is fated. As strength returns and makes Roy sob, the voice of the dwarf, Otto P. Zipp,
who has jeered Roy from the beginning of his career with the
Knights, rings out like a clarion: "Carrion, offal, turd—flush
the bowl" (223). The invective is an invitation to a personal
vendetta. "Choking up" on the bat, Roy smashes ball after ball
at the startled Zipp, anyone of which might have been a home
run. Moreover, the final foul ("Now I understand why they
call them fouls," Roy later declares [229]) strikes the dwarf's
head and careens upward to land in the face of Iris Lemon who
has come to tell Roy she is pregnant (smiling as the cycle of

her youth begins anew). Filled with sudden adoration, Roy bounds back onto the field determined to win. But he has lost already. The next blow, Brobdingnagian in power, not only goes foul but breaks Wonderboy in half. In the final inning, with a strange bat at his shoulder, Roy must face Herman Youngberry, the Pirate's star rookie who hopes someday to become a farmer. Looking now like Walter The Whammer, Roy strikes out with a roar. In a trice the fans and players vanish, and the wind wails forlornly through the bleachers.

Beyond this point there is for the ballplayer only the shattering realization of failure and the sense of future suffering. To be sure, the final chapter records a partial success: a confrontation with the unmasked Memo and her cohorts Gus Sands and Judge Banner. But, while Roy knocks the King of Bookies unconscious, pounds the judge until he has a bowel movement, and leaves Memo sobbing with rage, he departs in a cloud of self-hatred. On the street he must submit, as it is said that Shoeless Joe Jackson after the Chicago Black Sox scandal had to submit, to the sorrowing pleas of a newsboy: "Say it ain't true." But Roy, his ears still ringing with the lament of a passing woman that "He coulda been a king," can only weep and prepare himself for more of the random wandering which seems the special mark of spiritual "angst" for Malamud's father-seeking heroes (237).

V *The Pessimism of* The Natural

The Natural concludes, therefore, on a note of total loss. In this respect it serves, as many critics have noted, as a contrast to the more affirmative conclusions of the later novels. But the contrast is puzzling. At the end of the novel, Malamud allows Roy to fulfill many of the ritual requirements of the true hero, particularly the admission of love and the acceptance of fatherhood. That Roy is denied anything beyond this, therefore, reflects not only the hero's limitations but perhaps the limitations in the materials the author has chosen. In part, the conclusion is fated by virtue of Roy's narrowly conceived character. Part animal, part spirit (without a suggestion of intellect), the animal part of Roy's nature is so clearly predominant that success would have been totally unanticipated. But most importantly, given the nature of Malamud's beliefs, Roy Hobbes is doomed from the beginning; he is fated to failure by the very method the author employs. Despite the grotesque comedy and the metaphysical yoking of baseball and spiritual quest, Roy Hobbes is clearly the ancient hero, afoot in a dreamlike element, whose triumph would either reclaim the world itself or at least reverberate through all of society. Such a conclusion, in effect a "happy ending," would run counter to Malamud's sense of reality: to his belief that the forces of anti-life are at least as clear and powerful as the elusive humanity which resists them. Ultimately, success in Malamud can only occur when it is incomplete, sealed in irony and in a continuing, hallowing pain. Faced with pessimism of this order, Roy Hobbes can do nothing but fail.

Curiously, however, it is precisely Roy's dismal failure which also makes *The Natural* a clear introduction to the morality which informs Malamud's later work. In none other of his novels has he so directly, if abstractly, indicated the nature of the forces against which his later heroes must struggle, nor the ritual gestures by which they must preserve themselves. Not only is the capacity to suffer and to endure written large in the demands made upon Roy, but so also is the agonized determination to undergo death, or something very like death, in the tradition of heroic renewal. The successful resolution of the myth which controls *The Natural* demands that there be a deeply resisted moment when father and son, king and hero, end their separation; and the self, in torment, becomes its other. It is a "turning" rounded by further torment: to submit willingly to the loss of freedom and to resist the ego which divides man from his community.

Furthermore, *The Natural* displays with remarkable clarity an ironic portrayal of several traditional and more accessible agencies of transformation which also play a large role in the later novels. As Frank Kermode wrote, there are facts in all his novels which Malamud seems to hate; and the primary one seems to be that "It is, in the end, the fact of being alive that shuts you off from life."[12] What is most hard-headed about Malamud's moral dialectic (and what sets him apart from many of his contemporaries who also seek a way out of the underground) is his insistence—perhaps his Jewish insistence—that submission is the only avenue of redemption. The shibboleths of innocence and its related phenomenon, the celebration of the natural man, have only comic force in his works. And the comedy is constant. The longing for physical fulfillment besets all Malamud's heroes, whether they are imprisoned in concrete tenements or in their own divided psyches. For Roy Hobbes of *The Natural*, for Frankie Alpine of *The Assistant*, and climactically for S. Levin of *A New Life*, nature and sex hold out a freedom that promises an end to suffering. In all three novels, initial sexual acts are framed in pastoral settings—the image of a world free from the determinings of accident and history. When Memo climbs by accident into bed with Roy, the scene becomes, by virtue of the room's wallpaper, a venerable "Bower of Bliss": ". . . when she got into bed with him he almost cried out in pain as her icy hands and feet, in immediate embrace, slashed his hot body, but there among the apples, grapes, and melons, he found what he wanted and had it" (65). The vegetative setting, however, carries its own implicit deceit, as it does in *The Assistant*, where it becomes the background for a near-rape, and in *A New Life*, where it is only an extension of the university grounds. Memo's icy extremities are simply the mark of the devil; and in his struggle toward "natural" fulfillment, Roy, like S. Levin, finds himself thrust back into a more intense frustration than before.

Malamud's criticism of the myth of nature, or at least his insistence that the hero must triumph over nature, is clearly in the tradition of a people whose distrust of nature was always intense. It is also directly equated with the writer's refusal to succumb to the myth of innocence. The ancient cycle of son into father, hero into king, is the direct reverse of the romantic cycle; and Roy's boyhood, which in part carries the seeds of success, carries also its own formidable irony. Many of Roy's efforts to escape suffering take precisely the form of a quest for a return to childhood when he had not yet been called to a destiny that demanded succumbing to another. Thus the yearning for nature and for sex becomes in Malamud not only a desire for connection but, ironically, a mode of estrangement—an infantile regression not readily distinguishable from onanism. When Roy and Iris returned to the city from their evening at the beach, Iris had asked Roy to comfort her. When he refused, she had said, "When will you grow up, Roy?" (220), a line which is both a comment on the hero's limitations and an indication of his moral confusions. What had begun as an affair of the heart, the mark of which was the ease of the sex act, had become a conquest.

Conquest is not submission, of course, and the attainment of symbolic fatherhood demands, in all of Malamud's later novels, that sexual contact lead to a new relationship, one primarily nutritive. It is a truth which Roy, deep in his ambivalent heart, also recognizes. Late in the novel he has an impossible vision of his future with Memo; and, despite the fact that the dream is drenched in images of the fisher-king, the portrayal of imaginary happiness is unmistakably akin to the Jewish convention of the husband as "good provider":

> His heart ached the way he yearned for her (sometimes seeing her in a house they had bought, with a redheaded baby on her lap, and himself going fishing in a way that made it satisfying to fish, knowing that everything was all right behind him, and the home-cooked meal would be hot and plentiful, and the kid would carry the name of Roy Hobbes into generations his old man would never know. With this in mind he fished the stream in peace and later, sitting around the supper table, they ate the fish he had caught). . . . (179-80)

The "domestic" resolution of the ancient myth of the fisher-king, which in its traditional form leads to the marriage of the hero and his community, is, however, only a passing thought in Roy Hobbes's mind. In the history of Malamud's later heroes the primary form of the myth leads both Frankie Alpine and S. Levin out of estrangement and impotence and into dual roles as lover and father. But in any case, the process which turns the lover into a father is in all of Malamud's novels the basis for redemption generally; and in no case can it be altered. Before the hero can win through, he must submit to a final trial by love.

And trial by love is, by all odds, Malamud's fundamental subject. In his fictional world, as Jonathan Baumbach has stated, love is the only "redemptive grace—the highest good." And the "defeat of love, love rejected, love misplaced, love betrayed, loveless lust" are the primary evils.[13] Roy Hobbes's betrayals of his quest spring, of course, from all these corruptions, mirrored in his pursuit of Memo. However, his ultimate failure is his inability to accept Iris Lemon. For Iris, who reappears in three-dimensional form in the later novels—in Helen Bober and Pauline Gilley—holds out to the potential hero the form of his own ambivalence: the sweet and bitter lady, herself maimed by the world, who can be redeemed only by virtue of his love. Before he can take her, the lover must in effect renounce his ego and the mandates of the world which separate him from his heart. Similarly, for Frankie Alpine submission to love is tantamount to submission to imprisonment; to S. Levin it is equivalent to the renunciation of a new life. Before their final ironic redemption, both heroes undergo a cycle of comic despair that is echoed by most of the youthful heroes of Malamud's short stories. Deeply in love, they resist love with all their strength, just as Roy Hobbes resists it to the end of the novel. For it is only in the act of giving love that Malamud's heroes die to self and are reborn, despite their own limitations, to be something more than "other-directed" men. In all the novels and many of the short stories, the act of giving love is the final measure of a man's capacity for a free act. In choosing love, he selects the way of self-immolation and so flies in the face of all those "natural" voices which speak for peace, for success, for deceptive freedom.

VI *Malamud's Achievement*

Far from being incoherent, therefore, the ritual which mixes so strangely with the narrative of a baseball player (as Leslie Fiedler said, the "last symbol for the city-dweller of the heroic"[14]) supplies *The Natural* with a clear, telling vitality. In the finer passages, Roy Hobbes emerges as a lusty, perfectly viable image of present need. If his failures remind us of our limitations, his near success reminds us of the untapped resources for triumph which lie within. Though tormented by comic reversals and by the author's gloomy meditations, the book is from first to last a ballad of hope in which the most preposterous of subjects is fused to a vision that is, in most essentials, mystical and religious.

Furthermore, this attempt to enlist the resources of the "forgotten language" and to moderate it with a dazzling journalese also helps to account for the author's difficult achievement as well as his failings. So tenuous is the balance of idioms that it would be perhaps too demanding to expect *The Natural* to

be "all of a piece." Nor is it. The work is weakest in those
sections in which the metaphysical coupling of tongues prompts
Malamud into parody. Some of the more interesting portions
of *The Natural* are those scenes in which Roy descends into
a world of purely symbolic confrontation: the first meeting
with Judge Goodwill Banner in his tower, or the initial description of Pop Fisher. But while effective as comic allegory, they
ring of deliberate burlesque. Here for instance, are the comments of Judge Banner on the efficacy of darkness: "There is in
the darkness a unity, if you will, that cannot be achieved in any
other environment, a blending of the self with what the self
perceives, an exquisite mystical experience. I intend some day
to write a disquisition 'On the Harmony of Darkness; Can Evil
Exist in Harmony?' It may profit you to ponder the question"
(100).

While this passage evokes the spectre of "false" integration
(as well as the "monster of darkness" whose destruction is "the
hero's main feat")[15] it nonetheless seems all too evident; it is
almost as pat and easy as the first appearance of "Pop" Fisher,
who on a dry and dusty field is taking stock of himself: "I
shoulda been a farmer . . . I shoulda farmed since the day I
was born. I like cows, sheep, and those hornless goats—I am
partial to nanny goats, my daddy wore a beard—I like to feed
animals and milk 'em. I like fixing things, weeding poison oak
out of the pasture, and seeing to the watering of my crops" (45).

In passages such as these, the manipulation is all too
evident. At other times, the narrative is considerably weakened
by a self-indulgent tendency toward rhetorical sleight of hand.
If funny, the comedy depends upon stylistic jokes instead of the
"comedy of reversal" which Malamud, at his best, understands
to perfection. In *The Natural,* as in *The Assistant* and *A New Life,*
the most effective humor springs from a sudden unmasking in
which the hero's needs lead him into wild failures. When Roy
Hobbes, desperate for sexual contact, seeks to satisfy himself, he
seizes only a damaged breast. When, for his denial of Iris, he
feels an emptiness of spirit, he tries to assuage it through glut-
tony. Ultimately, such reversals lead him to a befuddled contact
with his own nakedness. In such scenes, laughter and terror con-
spire in an absurdity that is richly comic in the tradition of the
most ancient comedy which demands that man's efforts to deny

himself be met with laughter. But the humor is weakest, which is to say playful, when Malamud is most aware of the oddity of his subject and not its "naturalness." At such moments the writing becomes strained and collides, often directly, with the theme.

But such heavy-handedness is remarkably infrequent. What, in fact, is most distinctive about *The Natural* is that the author *has* managed to meld elements which seem utterly incompatible. The largest illustration of this is of course the very pattern of the work: the cross identification of mythic quest and baseball. But finally it is the poetry of the work, the creation of a deliberately impure yet perfectly organized style which charges the narrative with vitality. Throughout the book passages of idiomatic, terse, and slangy prose alternate with passages of lyrical intensity, and as often as not the two styles are prefectly integrated, even within the given sentence: "The long rain had turned the grass green and Roy romped in it like a happy calf in its pasture. The Redbirds, probing his armor, belted the ball to him whenever they could, which was often . . ." (83).

Such passages are no tour de force. They are instead the actualization of the basic tension of the book. The diction is as bifurcated as the hero it describes, carrying at one and the same time the elements of transcendence and defeat in heady suspension. At its most integrated, the opposition of myth and actuality, the rhythm of ecstasy and of the mundane, results in a tortured lyricism that lends even a batter's determination the grandeur of epic possibilities:

The ball appeared to the batter to be a slow spinning planet looming toward the earth. For a long light-year he waited for this globe to whirl into the orbit of his swing so he could burst it to smithereens that would settle with dust and dead leaves into some distant cosmos. At last the unseeing eye, maybe a fortune teller's lit crystal ball—anyway, a curious combination of circles—drifted within range of his weapon, or so he thought, because he lunged at it ferociously, twisting round like a top. He landed on both knees as the world floated by over his head and hit with a *whup* into the cave of Sam's glove. (29)

In large part this curious poetry dominates *The Natural*. In the scenes which record play or flight, self-confrontation or self-denial, the book throbs with a strange ambience composed of equal parts joke, mystery, and terror.

Moreover, the style imposes on the novel a sense of unreality which in itself suspends disbelief in much the same fashion a fairy tale does. Though the narrative smacks of stream-of-consciousness, only rarely can the reader tell if it is stream-of-consciousness in the mind of the character. Far closer to medieval romance than to the world of Joyce or Mann, to whom Malamud apparently owes his interest in mythic technique,[16] *The Natural* unfolds in a never-never land in which reality and unreality have been usurped by the patterns of imagery and by the style. If the novel seems at times a pure psychodrama, there are other moments when it seems like nothing so much as a romance intoned by a sports-minded Brooklyner.

Perhaps this fact more than any other serves to discriminate the literary manner of *The Natural* from that of the author's later novels. In *The Assistant* and in *A New Life* the ritual concerns of *The Natural* and the same "comi-tragic paradoxes of modern existence"[17] continue relatively unchanged. The major difference seems to be that the Jew in the later novels and stories summons up for Malamud the blighting materiality of a touchable and determining world with far more solidity than does *The Natural*. Compared to *The Natural*, in fact, *The Assistant* is a flatly realistic work. But this comparison is perilous, for it also obscures a good deal of similarity between the two books. For all its sense of a real world, the style of *The Assistant* is almost as dislocated and the presence of two voices is almost as manifest as in *The Natural*. The settings of *The Assistant* may *seem* durable; but, at the same time, they also seem to be fading into the mist.

What the course of Malamud's novels seems to suggest therefore is *not* the mechanical transition of a symbolist into a realist, but rather the development of an artist who has attempted to fuse these two traditions into a new style—not an impurity but a new manner. That Malamud is himself aware of this impulse seems clear from a recent address he made at Princeton University which was reported in *Esquire*:

Contrasting the present burgeoning of the poetic novel, which is accused of "never being violated by an idea," with a Dreiser-like concern in the past for "life in its beautiful materiality," he [Malamud] wound up with a statement of measured optimism to the effect that the novel of the future, though increasingly devoted to the handling of ideas, would not lose its present gains but would attain a new high ground "through the use of every imaginative resource at the writer's command" and thus achieve "more than the merely realistic."[18]

The sentence comparing the novel of ideas with the contemporary manner need not concern us. Malamud writes always of ideas. But what is most revealing about the statement is Malamud's concern for the "more than the merely realistic"—for a conception of the novel which unites the lyrical symbolism of the present with the resources of the naturalist-realist tradition. If this attitude rings naïvely of a "best of all possible worlds," it nonetheless helps to explain a good deal of the confusion which has been generated by criticism of Malamud. Despite the remarkable experimentation of *The Natural*, many critics persist in calling Malamud old-fashioned. Others see him as a writer in whom the demands of symbolism and realism exercise counter claims.[19] The truth, however, is that Malamud *is* a writer who has attempted to unite the realistic novel with the poetic and symbolic novel; and he has done so out of his very vision of the contemporary scene. Though he shares with a good many of his contemporaries the impulse to disregard the naturalistic manner, he has nonetheless resisted the impulse to disregard its truths. Though he believes always in the resources of the human spirit, he understands at the same time—perhaps with despair—the weight of determinism, of history, of accidents, and of social pressures which suffocate the spirit. In his best work, both these impulses fuse in a grotesque but powerful manner, in which affirmation is beset by irony, and horror by possibility. In the process, the reader is treated to the unsettling vision of a near-Dreiserian realism moderated and transmuted by a dedicated if existential belief in the heart's potential for success.

Needless to say, this fusion of theme and technique is as difficult to maintain as it is to describe. Assuredly Malamud has achieved his intention only rarely—at the most in a handful of stories and in his second novel; and these works are as inimitable as they are powerful. But those occasions when Malamud seems most unconvincing are often enough precisely those moments when he is unable to maintain this unity, when there is indeed an imbalance between the claims of symbolism and the claims of realism. This is exactly the problem in large sections of *A New Life* and many of the short stories, particularly those set in Italy.

However, this flaw is not quite the problem of *The Natural*, except as it pertains to lapses in the author's handling of language. From first to last, *The Natural* is a poetic and symbolic novel; and, as such, it is a prologue to his later work. Considered apart from *The Assistant* or *A New Life*, it is in fact uniquely impressive in its handling of paradox and in its employment of an accomplished and curiously fractured style. If the characters seem always more metaphorical than flesh-and-blood, they retain throughout, as Ben Siegel has indicated, "their human connections."[20] Dazzling as it must inevitably seem, *The Natural* makes the author's case in a manner totally unexpected and totally dramatic.

In truth, it is *only* in relation to Malamud's subsequent career that *The Natural* appears in any way lacking. Even at its finest, it is particularly deficient in conveying what the author's most powerful work always conveys: a sense of tangible reality, a wealth of "materiality" that gives authenticity to failure and to affirmation. Malamud's most precious work is always those stories in which the yearning for affirmation operates in the face of massive, countering determinisms and where the sense of "character," deeply felt, at once lends substance both to failure and to success. In *The Natural*, however, the exclusive reliance on poetry and pattern, and the denial by method of a *real* external world, make both failure and success too easy. At its worst, *The Natural* lacks conviction. At its best, it never quite becomes a deeply felt experience.

CHAPTER 3

The Assistant

"Love is responsibility of an *I* for a *Thou*."[1]
MARTIN BUBER

B ERNARD MALAMUD'S first book is concerned with its
hero's encounters in the public world; his second, *The
Assistant* (1957), is totally different. Opening in a tomb, *The
Assistant* closes in one: a wretched little grocery store in New
York City with an almost windowless five-room flat above. In
this soul-corroding twilight the principal characters have lived
for twenty-one years: Morris Bober, the aging and ailing store-
keeper who is the ethical center of the novel; his nagging wife
Ida who suffers from a weakness in the legs and the endurance
of her husband; and their twenty-three-year-old daughter, Helen,
who works for Levenspiel's Louisville Panties and Bras and
dreams of an escape from Bober fate. At the conclusion of the
first chapter a newcomer appears, a young Italian named Frankie
Alpine, who first robs Morris and then seeks to expiate his crime
by a descent into the store. Frankie's agony in the grocery, both
as assistant to Morris and as unlucky lover of Helen, supplies
the central drama in *The Assistant*.

That the Bobers' entombment makes for a depressing history
is clear to all readers of *The Assistant*. Every movement toward
freedom and every suffering cry consistently rebounds from the
shelves of canned goods to seal the unhappy victims in deeper
despair. In the two years which elapse in the narrative, it is only
occasionally that any of the characters can escape. Curiously
enough, what they encounter in these moments usually sends
them back to the store with mixed feelings of frustration and
release. For the truth of the matter is that, though they would
never admit it and cannot understand it, both Morris and Frankie
like the store.

[50]

Such refinement of masochism—and there is no other word for it—is in many ways unprecedented in American literature. And even if not quite unprecedented (there is always the darkly affirmative memory of Hawthorne), there still seems no way to classify *The Assistant* with any certainty. Read as a record of life tortured and withering under the weight of walls, poverty, and a hostile world, there has been nothing like *The Assistant* since Mike Gold angrily described the wails coming from New York's ghettos in the 1930's. One of the major differences, however, is that there is no anger in *The Assistant* on the part of the author and little withering on the part of the characters. If the Bober store is a grave, it is one in which, on occasion, people embrace.

I   The Assistant *Contrasted to* The Natural

Needless to say, little in *The Natural,* with its fixation on lyrical symbolism and on Roy's world-dissolving will, can quite prepare the reader for the suffocating intensities of *The Assistant.* Five years and a volume of short stories separate the two; but, read quickly and in order, one might suspect that the years were eras. As Malamud himself said of the work, "After completing my first novel, *The Natural,* in essence mythic, I wanted to do a more serious, deeper, perhaps realistic piece of work."[2] Despite the timeliness of the "perhaps," he succeeded. If not precisely in the tradition of naturalism, *The Assistant* still recalls the work of some of the great Jewish realists more clearly than it does the techniques of Joyce.

Unlike the fantastic adventures that accompanied Roy Hobbes's flight through space and time, *The Assistant* depicts life in which space and time seem irrelevant, suspended in the evocation of a gloomy everyday. The sense of human energy ground to static despair in a few disconsolate rooms is constant; and though rich in incident, events in the novel are so consistently underplayed by a tone of flat melancholy or ironic brevity that the reader is left finally not so much with a portrait of evolving history as with a blighting sense of routine. If a temporal universe even exists in *The Assistant,* it is hard to discover. Night gives way not to day but only to a night less dark, and the seasons play endless variations on a perpetual winter. If time promises the Bobers anything, it is only the constant anxiety of an insecure present extending backward and forward and usurping not only memory but hope. For Helen in her bedroom, wearily crossing off calendar days before they arrive, the future holds no promise at all; for Morris, yearning for his daily nap— "his one true refreshment"[3]—and reading yesterday's *Forward*, the future had long ago been interred in the grave of his young son Ephraim.

II *Frankie Alpine*

However, it is not alone the obvious contrast in mood and pace and the sense of a tangible environment which quickly tells the reader that *The Assistant* is a different kind of novel than *The Natural*. What persuades him of the fact is the sense of character in the work. Theodore Solotaroff said of the novel: "If *The Assistant* came as a revelation, as it did for me, partly the reason was that it restored a sense of the dynamics of character and of the older intention of fiction to show the ways men change. Despite its small compass and thinness of social reference, *The Assistant* could thus take on some of the power and clarity of the great 19th-century novels. . . ."[4]

Solotaroff's insight is correct, for it is substantially supported by Malamud's own contention that the chief business of the writer is "the drama of personality fulfilling itself."[5] The figures in *The Assistant* have an amplitude and concretion deeper than gesture and more complex than particular passions. Although Frankie Alpine and the Bobers are spilled on stage like the dregs of victimization, they pulsate with an ironic spirituality that suggests hope at the very moment their loneliness and frustrations seem beyond endurance. But it is Frankie Alpine and his progress and change from the day he first robs Morris to the day he assumes complete control of the store, which prompted Solotaroff's comment. Beyond the first chapter, the novel belongs to Frankie as *The Natural* belonged to Roy Hobbes, and for much the same reasons.

Indeed, what is most revealing about Malamud's depiction of his young Italian *isolato* is the manner in which he has transmuted the allegorical character of his earlier hero into a compellingly realistic one. Though the depth of his suffering obscures the fact, Frankie's agony is the same as the baseball player's. In his guilt-wracked efforts to escape the determinism of his own past and the countering claims of the will, the assistant confronts on almost every level, but in a new dimension, the same cycle of experience that shapes the morality of *The Natural*. In his first appearance in the book, having entered the Bober store with his accomplice and guide in crime, Ward Minoque, Frankie stands before a mirror which reflects not only a masked robber but an old man falling before a blow from Ward's pistol. In the conjunction of saintly grocer and hate-filled criminal, both of whom obscure Frankie's own terror-stricken face, the future assistant sees the emblems of his own disparate nature and his ultimate burden.

Frankie's past, moreover, is also a teasing mystery that is conveyed through a series of images sufficient only to indicate the sources of his anxiety and his motivation. Rather than a coherent record, the assistant's history before his apprenticeship resolves itself finally into a pattern of knotted memories of want and failure that are further obscured by guilt. At one point in the novel, "rehearsing" a confession to Morris, Frankie indicates the nature of his earlier experiences in a passage rendered almost meaningless by shame:

> . . . after certain bad breaks through various causes, mostly his own mistakes—he was piled high with regrets—after many such failures, though he tried every which way to free himself from them, usually he failed; so after a time he gave up and let himself be a bum. He lived in gutters, cellars if he was lucky, slept in lots, ate what the dogs wouldn't or couldn't, and what he scrounged out of garbage cans. He wore what he found, slept where he flopped and guzzled anything. (91)

Frankie's incoherence is only the dramatic tissue of what is perhaps the most persuasive element in the characterization. From his first appearance in the novel, the clerk's agony occurs in a strange emotional borderland where he feels more than he expresses and, strangely, expresses more than he immediately feels. Though he has come to the East from the West Coast in order to gain more of the world, it is clear that the journey is, like Roy's, a symbolic translation of the heart's search for a new life. Though Frankie fails to understand the nature of his past, his passion is to change it: "to clean it out of his self and bring in a little peace . . . to change the beginning" (90). Like Stephen Daedelus, another Catholic in search of an unacknowledged Jewish father, Frankie, had he been an intellectual, might have cried: "History is a nightmare from which I am trying to awake." And throughout his development, the sense of past and continuing failures conflict with other images of the past, particularly the memories of stories of St. Francis which had been taught him as a youth in a Catholic orphanage. "He said poverty was a queen and he loved her like she was a beautiful woman," Frankie explains to Sam Pearl, the candy-store owner, the day after his crime against Morris. "Every time I read about somebody like him I get a feeling inside of me I have to fight to keep from crying. He was born good, which is a talent if you have it" (31).

Frankie's worship of St. Francis and his addiction to stories dealing with the saint's gentleness serve as the ironic basis for his transformation into a Jew. Equally important, his worship also deciphers the riven nature of his personality. In the ironic juxtaposition of persona in his first and second appearances in the novel—masked criminal in one, saint worshipper in the other—Malamud indicates the need for integration which animates not only Frankie's history in the store but the crime which precipitated it. For Malamud, as for Dostoevsky, whom he much resembles, the ambiguous agony in which ego and alterego collide is the most fertile of all subjects. Though tempered by satire and realism, the issue in *The Assistant* is in a way sainthood or villainy, hero or non-hero—in any case, the outer limits of personality yearning to resolve itself. The "way" of the criminal is therefore not so much different from the "way" of the saint; it is its paradoxical brother.

What distinguishes Frankie's experiences is what Unamuno has somewhere called a "furious appetite for being," and the measure of his appetite is his ambivalence. "He was like a man with two minds" (122), Malamud writes; and the pain of this state is registered in scenes of self-loathing and, frequently, physical pain. When in the role of crime-expiating clerk, Frankie steals from Morris' register, he suffers for the act a headache so intense that "He was afraid to look into the mirror for fear it would split apart and drop into the sink" (85). While it is futile and misleading to speak of *definitive* identity, Frankie, during his whirling progress, alternates with furious rapidity from lover to hater, victim to victimizer, and saint to criminal. And the short history of his life in the store is continually dominated by the yearning of a fractured personality to resolve and so "fulfill itself": first as exiled criminal and then, inchoately, as Ganymede to Ganymede, servant to servant.

To round out his distinctive themes—again an echo of *The Natural*—Malamud suggests that alienation from self is the grounds of isolation from other men. The measure of Frankie's "fulfillment," his potential for victory, is inevitably equated with his submission to others, to a will-breaking responsibility. When Frank enters the Bober grocery as penitent, he tells Morris: "I don't understand myself. I don't really know what I'm saying to you or why I am saying it" (37). A moment before he had said the same thing in another form: "What I mean to say is that when I need it most something is missing in me, in me or on account of me. I always have this dream where I want to tell somebody something on the telephone so bad it hurts, but then when I am in the booth, instead of a phone being there, a bunch of bananas is hanging on a hook" (37).

That Malamud might be indebted to Dostoevsky for his concept of isolation as a mode of inhuman determinism is suggested by certain parallels to *Crime and Punishment*. Like Raskolnikov, the seeds of Frankie Alpine's crime have been nourished by self-incarceration; and the justification for his crime is a twin to the Russian student's—an attempt to destroy the countering claims of the self by an act of "negative self-determinism." The description of Frankie's decision sounds, in fact, like a mocking summary of Raskolnikov's:

> But one day while he lay in some hole he had crawled into, he had this terrific idea that he was really an important guy, and was torn out of his reverie with the thought that he was living this kind of life only because he hadn't known he was meant for something a whole lot better—to do something big, different. He had not till that minute understood this. In the past he had usually thought of himself as an average guy, but there in this cellar it came to him that he was wrong. That was why his luck had so often curdled, because he had the wrong idea of what he really was and had spent all his energy trying to do the wrong things. Then when he had asked himself

what should he be doing, he had another powerful idea, that
he was meant for crime. He had at times teased himself with
this thought, but now it wouldn't let go of him. At crime he
would change his luck, make adventure, live like a prince.
(91-92)

And the parallels are enforced by frequent ironic asides. When
Helen discovers Frankie in the nearby public library and asks
what he is reading, he tells her *The Life of Napolean*. And he
adds: "Why not—he was great, wasn't he?" (97).

If inadvertently satirical, the echoes of *Crime and Punishment*
are surprisingly obviated by the fullness with which Malamud
has plotted Frankie's character. For his crime—even if *only*
against a Jew (and Frankie's choice of victim, like Raskolnikov's,
is an ironic commentary on his motivation), the assistant must
submit to profound spiritual anxiety. His return to the scene of
the crime on the following day, and his desperate attempts to
find work as Morris' assistant, even though unwanted, have all
the nightmarish authenticity of Dostoevsky's guilt-tortured souls.
Similarly, Frankie's efforts to *lead* himself into penitential suffering ring convincingly like those half-demented figures in the
Russian novelist's world for whom self-induced torture is an
emblem of their goodness and proof they are on the right path.
"When I don't feel hurt," Frankie one day proclaims to Helen,
"I hope they bury me" (116).

The framework which directs Frankie's development throughout the ten chapters of the novel, however, seems less a direct
appropriation from Dostoevsky than a parallel of the history
of the Jews themselves—a pattern that Malamud has described
as "First, the Prophets' 'way of gentleness;' the Sins of the People,
Punishment, Exile and Return . . . the primal problem of man
seeking to escape the tragedy of the past."[6] The first chapter
of *The Assistant,* a recounting of a typical Morris Bober day,
ends with Frankie's crime. The next five chapters belong to
Frankie's punishment. At the conclusion of the second chapter,
the young Italian dons Morris' apron and explains only, "I need
the experience" (54). The line signals both his defeat and his
salvation: the half-understood acceptance of the victim's identity
and all the enraging frustration that goes with it. Frankie's
punishment, however, hides progress at the same time it mys-

teriously forwards it. Initially, he succumbs to his bewildering motivation with a sense of relief; he welcomes the store's solidity, its separation from the outside world. But almost immediately his victimization—his Jewish victimization—asserts itself clearly. To his compound of human needs the store gives nothing. Though he struggles continuously with the desire to confess to Morris, he retreats constantly from the thought of the "Jew listening with a fat ear" (157). On his first day in the store he returns the seven dollars which he stole; but a short time later, and though it is only through his efforts that the Bobers can meet expenses, he begins to steal from the register—at first occasionally and then with grinding regularity. What is worse, for stealing he must suffer not only the "smell" of his own decay but at times a "curious pleasure" (69).

The significance of Frankie's complex pains is clear, however. In suffering for his relapses and for his joy at his relapses, Frankie undergoes changes which in time will transform him into a Jew. Ironically, it is precisely this fact which neither Frankie nor Morris can quite understand. Perhaps the grimmest humor in the novel springs from the assistant's and the proprietor's efforts to deny a relationship that is apparent in every gesture; both retreat into a complex prejudice that perpetually screens their merging humanity. "You had to be a Jew," despairs Frankie in the midst of his grinding assistantship. "They were born prisoners" (86). "Who could stay in such a place but a goy whose heart was stone?" reflects Morris late in the novel (195). In an ambiguous drama of cross purposes that do not really cross, Malamud indicates the unacknowledged relationship that unites the pair.

In his first conversation with the grocer, Frankie's recital of his past failures causes Morris to think: "I am sixty and he talks like me" (37). Later, when Frankie reads a copy of *Crime and Punishment* given him by Helen, he is disturbed and "repelled . . . with everybody in the joint confessing to something every time he opened his yap. . . . Frankie first had the idea he [Raskolnikov] must be a Jew." A moment later, the author relates how Frankie had the "crazy sensation that he was reading about himself" (107-8). Though Frankie denies it to the last moment, as does Morris, his transformation from anti-Semite to Jew is continuous. Retreating from Bober's sympathy he castigates the old man internally: "His pity leaks out of his pants" (83). And, rising at dawn to tend the store with a zeal that can only be compensated for by theft—an act which rebounds like a knife into his own heart—Frankie cries passionately: ". . . a Jew is a Jew. . . . What the hell are they to me so that I gave them credit for it?" (70) Throughout the first half of the novel—the record of his punishment—Frankie and Morris, in the seemingly inviolable separateness of Jew and Goy, bound and rebound upon each other without really knowing it; and in the process Frankie's identity is worn away, later to be refashioned.

III *Helen Bober*

To further the dramatic tension in the assistant's development into a Jew, Malamud has written into the novel a symbolic parallel to the Frankie-Morris relationship. Ward Minoque, Frank's accomplice in the crime and a consummate Jew hater, represents the polarity of the assistant's character: Ward is Frankie's Svidrigailov. Similarly, Ward's relationship to his father, the detective of the story, represents a reverse variation of the symbolic father-son relationship. Motivated by his own stern conception of the law, legal rather than moral, Detective Minoque searches after Ward continuously in an effort to drive him from the neighborhood; and, just as continuously, Ward flees punishment. It is Ward who, sensitive to all things Jewish, recognizes Frankie's initial change and delivers judgment on it: "You stinking kike" (145).

In the same scene, Ward hits a second mark. Mocking Frank's efforts in the store, he says "Your Jew girl must be some inspiration" (144). Ward's reference is to Helen Bober, who like some damaged Sophie, both animates the assistant's quest for rebirth and challenges it. In Helen, who has spent twenty-one of her twenty-three years in the grave of a store, Malamud has enlarged the image of Iris Lemon in the form of an aching dissatisfaction, in which unfulfilled desires induce both lethargy and hysterical pride. "I won't [compromise] with my ideals" (45), Helen proclaims to Louis Karp; but, for Helen, ideals serve the purposes of anti-life and self-delusion.

At the heart of Helen's character is a complex, dividing hurt. Dramatically, she unites, as Jonathan Baumbach has noted, all the "sons" of the novel—Louis Karp; Nat Pearl, the Columbia law student; Ward Minoque; and Frankie—into a single contrasting unit.[7] But like the group itself, her personality is a shambles. Poverty and an unremitting drabness have induced in her a yearning for some impossible fulfillment, a future outside the store in which her plea—"Life *has* to have some meaning"—can be realized (43). In the static round of work, sleep, and needs unsatisfied, her life turns upon a desperate hunger for an end to a never-ending winter, for a future which robs her of the present. "What am I saving myself for . . . What unhappy Bober fate?" Helen asks herself (46).

Malamud's manipulation of the Helen-Frankie relationship involves the reader in perhaps the most ambiguous thematic issues in the novel. Unwillingly, Helen finds herself both interested in and repelled by Frankie. His following eyes suggest both danger and a gratifying adoration; and her reaction is further compounded by her mother's attempts to keep them apart, by Frankie's non-Jewishness and by, ironically, the very nature of his reclamation—his future as another Morris. There is also a sense of physical danger; for sex, Helen believes, has betrayed her. She had lost her virginity long ago with Nat Pearl, "handsome, cleft-chinned, gifted, ambitious," who "had wanted without too much trouble a lay and she, half in love, had obliged and regretted." Later, "unwillingly willing she had done it again." In retreat from experience and from her own awareness that she had wanted a stake in Nat's future (for Helen, like Frankie, is inevitably better than she thinks), Helen seeks refuge in an abstract, programmatic assault on her destiny: ". . . she promised herself next time it would go the other way; first mutual love, then loving, harder maybe on the nerves, but easier in memory" (14). In the meantime, her emotions stalled, she dreams of attending night courses at college and reads endlessly.

However, what Helen retreats from is the disintegrating power of love. Unconsciously drawn to Frank, and recognizing that in the palpable hunger of his spirit there exists resources which Nat lacks she unconsciously manipulates the reality of his person into "possibilities" dead to her father—into a future which might also be hers: ". . . don't make a career of a grocery," she tells him. "There's no future in it" (96). And, locked in her own dichotomy, she refuses his gifts with a fragment of her mother's wisdom—"For gifts you pay" (112); at the same time she heaps upon him ambitions which deny the very nature of his quest and the very resources which attract her.

IV *The Role of Love in* The Assistant

Confusions such as these dominate Helen's bouts with love from beginning to end. And the mixture in Frankie is doubly intense; for while his need for love is as insupportable as it was for Roy Hobbes, it is marked throughout by the same duality of purpose which undercuts his relationship to the grocery and to Morris. In fact, the union of criminal and saint, clerk and robber, is matched by the role of lover as luster and lover as provider, by the lover as romantic and as sensualist. In a brilliant scene, devastating in its compression, Frankie one day climbs the dumb-waiter to spy on Helen in her bathroom. Stilling the voice which tells him that "if you do it . . . you will suffer," he gazes at a body which before his eyes transpires, or is redeemed, into something more than flesh: "Her body was young, soft, lovely, the breasts like small birds in flight, her ass like a flower." At the same time, however, he realizes that "in looking he was forcing her out of reach, making her into a thing only of his seeing, her eyes reflecting his sins, rotten past, spoiled ideals, his passion poisoned by his shame" (74-76).

The collision of images, however, is part of the dialogue of redemption which is constant in the novel; and of Frankie's development through love there can be no doubt. With remarkable foreshortening, sometimes only a gesture, Malamud indicates that his rebirth through suffering is continued and invigorated by love, which seems finally the only means of breaking through the barriers of self. Nearing the end of his period of punishment, Frankie one day listens to Helen's reminder of what separates them: "Don't forget I'm a Jew." His response, simplistic as a child's, heralds the breakthrough of spirit: "So what?" he replies (121). In apparently accidental exchanges such as these, or in the ironic transposition of voices, Frankie's ritual success is artfully elaborated. Moreover, his growth proves to be a reclamation of Helen herself, who "despite the strongest doubts" (130) finds herself falling in love with the assistant at the same time that she retreats from Nat Pearl, the symbolic realization of a non-Bober future.

Indeed, before all progress finally dissolves in the terrors of accident and in the last gesture of a hungering will, Helen sees in Frankie, though hardly aware of it, the concrete emblems of his secret nature—Frankie Alpine in the guise of his namesake, Francis of Assisi, communing with the birds:

> Coming up the block, Helen saw a man squatting by one of the benches, feeding the birds. Otherwise, the island was deserted. When the man rose, the pigeons fluttered up with him, a few landing on his arms and shoulders, one perched on his fingers, pecking peanuts from his cupped palm. Another fat bird sat on his hat. (118)

So much at least Malamud allows to Frankie's development in his attempt to recapitulate in the character's life the drama of man "seeking to escape the tragedy of the past." But beyond this point, as Ihab Hassan notes, "ambiguities prevail."[8] Before Frankie can re-enact the parable of Jewish history, punishment must give way to exile; and, in a sudden reversal, Frankie and Morris Bober plunge into the world of fortuity and misunderstanding. Despite the assistant's plea that he "was a different person now," (198) the weight of accident contradicts every gesture and carries with it any shred of sentimentalism that might have inhered in the earlier sections.

The chapter recording the beginning of Frankie's exile is underscored by irony. Having lured Helen into his small bedroom, he hears her plea that "I want to be disciplined, and you have to be too if I ask it," with a startled sense of understanding (140). Alone in the store, he empties some of the stolen cash from his wallet into the register and "with a surge of joy" rings up a no-sale; he thinks that now he will control his life, shape it, "clean up the slate in a single swipe" (157-58). But a moment later Helen calls and begs him to meet her that evening in the park, pleading the arrival of spring and promising the clerk, or so he believes, the physical fulfillment she has refused him. For all his sense of remorse, Frankie takes back a dollar from the register in order to bring Helen home in a cab. The conflict of values, however, precipitates ruin at the same time that it invokes success. Frankie's theft is quickly discovered by Morris,

BERNARD MALAMUD

whose suspicions of the assistant had long ago been aroused. Though moved by Frankie's frenzied pleas to let him remain, Morris thinks of Helen and refuses with a groan to extend any more trust to the clerk.

At the back of Morris' denial, however, is something more complex than his concern for Helen—though it is that too. It is further the never recognized despair at the knowledge—imparted by his landlord Karp—that external conditions, not the clerk, were responsible for the sudden success of the store. Grief-stricken, the old grocer watches his clerk hang up his apron and leave to wander the streets or to stare at himself with "nose-thumbing revulsion" (174). And the irony is triply compounded. Now certain he will lose Helen, Frankie enters the spring-touched park vowing to "love her with his love," and so convince her of the purity of his claim (175). But Helen, hurrying in an anticipation that was intensified by weariness of anticipation, had arrived in the park minutes before. Instead of Frankie she finds Frankie's shadow. To her horror, Ward Minoque materializes before the bench on which she sits. "All I want is what you give that wop," Ward cries; and Helen, thrown to the ground, struggles in delirium until Ward is seized from behind by Frankie and then, chased away, re-emerges as the clerk who stops her "pleas with kisses." Afterwards, Helen's fascinating wail rings through the park and adds to Frankie's self-incarceration the hatred of ages: "Dog—uncircumcised dog!" (167-68).

Though motivated by a rape that was not a rape, Helen's ritual cry creates a period of profound confusion. In every direction, the sense of agony increases. The store itself is threatened with instant ruin; it is crushed by the competition of a new delicatessen around the corner. Morris in his bedroom yearns for death; Frankie in his is being killed by his thoughts. In swift alterations of scene, horror gives way to horror: from Helen endlessly showering to wash away the assistant's touch—though in reality to divert hatred from herself; then to Morris and to Frankie; and then again back to Helen. This endless wheel of remorse has its first concrete actualization in Morris' "accidental" brush with death when he falls asleep with the stopcock of the radiator open. Rescued by Frankie, the grocer is taken to the hospital and remains there with pneumonia.

The only directive impulse in these few remaining chapters belongs to Frankie, whose passion to remain in the store—now that Morris is absent—becomes not so much heroic as maniacal. With a determination that is proof even against Helen's hatred, he labors incessantly, repainting, revarnishing, re-arranging, vowing that "they would carry him out in a box" (192). All his work, however, brings in not a single new customer. In the end, Frankie takes a job as counterman in an all-night coffee shop; he works there from the moment the grocery closes until dawn when he returns to the store to sell the three-cent, unseeded roll to the "Poilesheh" who comes by every morning. In the face of his self-abasement even Ida relents somewhat in her suspicion of the "goy"; she weeps when she one day comes into the kitchen to see him preparing a lunch of boiled potatoes: "Why do you work so hard for nothing? What do you stay here for?" Frankie reflects: "For love" (187).

Curiously—and horribly—it is not Ida now but Morris, when he returns from the hospital, who is determined that the clerk should not remain. Even the assistant's confession of his initial crime is unavailing. Though he tells Morris the truth, and for reward experiences "a moment of extraordinary relief—a treeful of birds broke into song," Frankie has to withstand the last unutterable indignity. "This I already know," Morris replies; "you don't tell me nothing new" (198).

The mythic quest for fatherhood has been subverted in the early chapters by the character of the hero himself, but it collapses in the last sections under the weight of irony, accident, and, climactically, Morris Bober's own obdurate blindness—a blindness which exacts from him the full measure of suffering. Indeed, in the final two chapters myth and non-myth collide with such force that the narrative becomes at times almost surrealistic. His exile apparently complete, Frankie re-connects with Morris only twice: first, in the form of the unwanted son when he rescues the grocer and the store from a fire which Morris had started to collect insurance money; later, when he attends Morris' funeral and dances out, to the horror of the assembled mourners, his unacknowledged transformation. Bending over the grave to follow the course of Helen's thrown rose, he loses his balance and lands on the coffin. When Ida and Helen return to their airless apartment from the cemetery, the first sound they hear is the ring of the register that informs them that the "grocer was the one who had danced on the grocer's coffin" (232).

V Morris Bober's Identity

What follows, in a single short chapter, is both summary and apotheosis. In this epilogue, Malamud quickly traces the second of Frankie's years in the store; and, for all its disconsolate ironies, he affirms the clerk's return and his assumption of Bober's identity. But what supports and finally convinces us of Frankie Alpine's "wretched" triumph, his return to the "Prophets' way of gentleness," is the identity of the prophet himself. To understand Frankie's conversion, it is necessary, therefore, to understand this hapless engineer of human potential who, like a Sisyphus in slow motion, makes believable the vision that goodness can be proof against the exigencies of the world and of history.

Morris Bober's portrait is the author's triumph. In creating him, Malamud relied less on the mythic image of the son-seeking father in *The Natural* than on a perhaps analogous but infinitely more human tradition which extends backward to Job. In some respects, Morris is a quintessential instance of the Jewish "sufferer" whose enemy is life itself—or, at least, every impulse of inhumanity which naturalism, as well as the tragic vision, has isolated and decried; and they zero in on his goodness like flies to honey. At times the novel seems to become an enormous joke in which nature and fate, far from being "disinterested," take active delight in torturing the grocer, secure in the knowledge that he, with "the will of a victim," will submit with only a murmur (206).

What preserves the portrait of Morris Bober from sentimentality and turns him into Malamud's most impressive character stems from two sources. One is simply Malamud's relentlessness: his refusal to mitigate Morris' pain. The pattern of turnabout which dominates Morris' life is consistently far-ranging, undercutting every hope. It had been so from his first days in America. As a young man in night school, Morris at one point recalls, he had learned a scrap of poetry: " 'Come,' said the wind to the leaves one day,/'come over the meadow with me and play' " (83). The line lingers on in constant references to the wind which, however, never plays with Morris: instead, it pursues him. In the opening of the novel, the grocer descends the steps at dawn to enact the daily ritual of hauling in the milk cases and selling a three-cent roll. The season is fall. In reality it is winter:

> The early November street was dark though night had ended, but the wind, to the grocer's surprise, already clawed. It flung his apron into his face as he bent for the two milk cases at the curb. Morris Bober dragged the heavy boxes to the door, panting. A large brown bag of hard rolls stood in the doorway along with the sour-faced, gray-haired Poilisheh huddled there, who wanted one. (3)

This paragraph, the first in the novel, abstracts what is to be the final horror of Morris' predicament: dispossessed of nature, he retreats into a store which represents a deeper dispossession. Moreover, the "surprise" Morris feels at the touch of the cold wind is echoed again and again in the novel. Nature in *The Assistant* offers less release than in *The Natural,* and the anti-romantic irony haunts the experience of all the characters— no matter how romantic their sensibilities. Though Morris, like Helen, yearns for spring, for the promise of rebirth, both are continually tortured by a "false spring," by an April which is assuredly the cruelest month of all. The promise of spring leads Helen to rape, Morris to death. On the final day of his life, the suddenly jovial grocer goes out to clear the walkway of an unseasonable April snow and thus precipitates the heart attack which kills him. "What kind of winter," he asks, "can be in April?" (223).

This question is purely rhetorical; at most, it is slightly indignant. For Morris Bober "knows his fate." Yet this knowledge bears its own measure of agony. Morris' insight is futile: he seems in fact a man who cannot learn from experience. Though he should not hope, he persists in doing so. In return, the world cries "Surprise!"—and stabs him again. As numerous critics have pointed out, Morris is a hero of endurance—a man painfully, even pridefully aware of the tragic undercurrents of human existence. But what Morris Bober endures is only himself. His weary "Oi" may be a comment on the horror of his life, his wife's suffering, his daughter's loss of childhood; but most importantly it is the guilty acknowledgment that the nature of his own soul has brought these things about.

Morris' victimization by life, moreover, is matched by his victimization by author—perhaps the most terrible aspect of his ordeal. For Malamud allows his saintly hero no relief at all. More spectacle than consciousness, the grocer stumbles and weaves through the novel in an eternal punishment, most of it self-induced, to die without awareness of his own value. "I gave away my life for nothing," is Morris' final reflection. Malamud adds: "It was the thunderous truth" (226). Even compassion is not accorded Morris. Every attempt at tragic declamation, or even tragic presence, is denied him from the beginning. When Morris lights a cigarette and suffers a fit of coughing, Malamud writes only: "He coughed harshly, his face lit like a tomato" (7). When at the end of the first chapter, a synoptic review of a lifetime of failure, Morris falls before Ward's blow, Malamud sums up the event in a sentence of weirdly effective understatement: "The end fitted the day. It was his luck, others had better" (27).

Such understatement denies the reader any relief. One of the most depressing qualities in *The Assistant*, in fact, stems from the author's refusal to mitigate Morris' suffering through recourse to emotional rhetoric or by giving the character some awareness of the beauty of his ways. The reality of Morris' relationship to Frankie, for instance, is never understood by either character. For the old grocer, it seems only a preparation for more pain and more treachery. Even Helen's thoughts on the day of her father's funeral give the memory of Bober nothing: "I said Papa was honest but what was the good of such honesty if he couldn't exist in the world?" (230). As for Frankie, even though he tumbles into Morris' grave, the death of the grocer was no cause for lament: "He felt a loss but it was an old one" (228). Each of the characters, as Solotaroff notes, is locked within the prison of his own suffering;[9] and the narrative pattern makes this clear. The focus in *The Assistant*, disjunctive to an almost playful degree, switches unexpectedly from one character to another but rarely settles on two at once. The answer to the question of why men suffer lies locked in the mystery of human relations. Despite the constriction of the grocery, however, Malamud refuses, except to illustrate misunderstanding, to allow one character passage into the realm of another. If the reader senses, as he does, the common center of their needs, the characters themselves do not.

But, if the unrelieved intensity of suffering helps to save Morris Bober from bathos, the comic spectacle of his suffering makes him unforgettable. "Leid macht auch Lachen"—sorrow also creates laughter—an old Jewish proverb insists, and the line serves as a final commentary on the source of affirmation in *The Assistant* and Morris' role in that affirmation. That is to say, if the grocer is in the tradition of Job, he is also a member in high standing of another old tradition: that of the *shlemihl*, or "holy" innocent, who for a millennium has been one of the prime agencies in transforming exile into sainthood.

Half ironic, half absurd, Morris is patently one of those absurb emblems of Jewish "luck" who finds that the clock stops when he winds it or the chicken walks when he slays it. From first to last, the grocer's victimization wears the form of comic reversal. Perhaps the most persistent of the jokes springs from Morris' relationship to Karp, his landlord and a successful liquor-store owner. When Karp fears a robbery, it is Morris who is robbed; when Morris yearns for a fire and the insurance money, it is Karp's store which burns. That Karp proves in the end to be a *victim* of success, yearning unconsciously to be Morris, only adds sting to the humor.

But perhaps the wriest jokes spring from Malamud's parody of the typical American success story which he dresses up in a motley of Jewish and American features. For all his accent, Morris' honesty is Lincolnesque. An anecdote has it that, once in the middle of winter, "without hat or coat, without rubbers to protect his feet," Morris ran for two blocks to return a nickel to a customer (228). But such honesty has brought the grocer only further entombment. Similarly, whenever Morris dreams of freedom, of the promise of space, he has no resource but memories of childhood, of the Russia he had to flee as a youth. This is a joke which even Frankie can understand: "He had escaped out of the Russian Army to the USA, but once in a store he was like a fish fried in deep fat" (83).

If the irony is reminiscent of anything, it is of an old movie which Charlie Chaplin (himself a modern instance of the *shlemihl*[10]) appeared in, called *The Immigrant*. A shipload of ragged voyagers from Eastern Europe, Chaplin among them, line the rail to cheer the Statue of Liberty. Across the screen flashes the announcement "The Land of the Free." But, as the camera again takes over, a burly guard is encircling the refugees with a chain.

It is, however, the source of the jokes which remind the reader of the full intent of the comedy. As Theodore Reik states in his study of Jewish wit, the *shlemihl* "is the hidden architect of his misfortune," a masochist who finds in suffering the conditions of victory.[11] Morris' chief burden, as we have seen, is himself: his own obdurate saintliness. But, whenever he chooses to escape himself, whenever he succumbs to his own "opposing self," he immediately suffers reversal. When, through the agency of Julius Karp, a potential buyer appears in the person of a fresh-faced smiling refugee, Morris teeters between the hope of a final escape from the store and his own pained conscience. At the last moment, he cannot be dishonest. Despite Ida's cries of warning, he tells the refugee what the store is like and in a moment is "swimming in his sea of woes" (203). The buyer flees. Later in the novel Morris encounters his most definitive alterego in the person of a red-haired *macher* (manipulator) who urges the grocer to hire him to burn the store and collect the insurance money. Though Morris sends the devilish vision away, he decides for the fire. But no sooner does it begin than he finds that not only the store is afire but his own person is as well. The comedy in *The Assistant* appears, in other words, whenever Morris seeks to slight his real identity—whenever he forgets, as Isaac Rosenfeld said of Sholom Aleichem's comic heroes, that "the only trustworthy and familiar . . . locus of values" is suffering.[12] In this respect the laughter serves in the capacity of redemptive emotion; it is a reminder that the way to transcendence lies only through the ability to endure privation.

Finally, it is only because of their endurance and their privation that Morris Bober and Frankie Alpine sense that they are true to themselves. But this realization also carries its measure of comic relief, for what the characters sense is not the same as what they understand. This fact underscores Frankie's ambiguous contempt for Morris. Though Frankie himself actively seeks pain as the one sensible reminder that he is "on the way," the assistant nonetheless condemns the process in Morris and in Jews generally: "That's what they live for, Frank thought, to suffer. And the one that has got the biggest pain in the gut and can hold onto it the longest without running to the toilet is the best Jew. No wonder they got on his nerves" (88).

Frankie's comment is not wrong; it is only incomplete. In some ways Morris is the prototype of that army of ragged Jews, almost all of them refugees and almost all of them old, who in Malamud's stories—though in none other of his novels—unwittingly proclaim the efficacy of suffering. In them the sense of Jewish tradition, rather than its form, lives close to the surface; and this tradition motivates their agony. But their suffering is never, as Frankie believes, an end in itself. It is instead, as Iris Lemon had put it, the agency which "teaches us to want the right things"; it is a decision, if an unconscious one, for the pained crucible out of which principles of conduct are dignified and authenticated.

VI *The Moral Basis of* The Assistant

The theme of redemptive suffering in *The Assistant* is thus clearly akin to that of *The Natural*. But, unlike his first novel, Malamud supports the concept in *The Assistant* not with an ancient mythic ritual but with Talmudic ethics. At one point in the novel, Morris tells Frankie that the "Jewish Law" is the basis of his behavior—not the word but the law. "Nobody," he says, "will tell me that I am not Jewish because I put in my mouth once in a while, when my tongue is dry, a piece ham. But they will tell me, and I will believe them, if I forget the Law." The nature of that law, as Morris defines it, consists of moral principles which, on the surface, sound simplistic in the extreme: "This means to do what is right, to be honest, to be good. This means to other people. Our life is hard enough. Why should we hurt somebody else? For everybody should be the best, not only for you or me. We ain't animals. This is why we need the Law. This is what a Jew believes" (124). Later, at Morris' burial, a mysterious rabbi echoes the grocer's morality and dignifies it with oratory: "Morris Bober was to me a true Jew because he lived in the Jewish experience, which he remembered, and with the Jewish heart" (229).

But if simplistic in presentation, there is nothing simple about Morris' adherence to principle, for it is tested in a world so complex and so redolent with reversal and pain that it is at times difficult to gauge success from failure. Morris Bober's lacks become, whether acknowledged or not, everybody's gains. To win, in Malamud's universe, is also to lose. As Solotaroff has strikingly indicated, "It is Malamud's pessimism that has allowed him to make convincing the main idea that a man is not necessarily bound within his limits."[13] And the record of Bober's pain illustrates this point. To suffer out of love and principle is to see the ego die and the self dissolve in the terror of complete dispossession. "I suffer," Morris tells Frankie, "for you." And when Frankie, in aching bewilderment, asks what Morris means, he can only prophesy the assistant's own victory: "I mean you suffer for me" (125). Like one of the thirty-six Just Men in the Jewish legend of the Lamed Vov—saints who are often unaware of their station, but whose number is ceaselessly replenished by ritual replacement—Morris Bober suffers for all. He is a receptacle of pain without which "humanity would suffocate with a single cry."[14] Or, as Malamud himself says of Bober: "The world suffers. *He* felt every schmerz" (7).

Ultimately, at the heart of Frankie's conversion—as well as Morris Bober's identity—is a transcendent mystery. But, curiously, there are none of the features of mystery. Assuredly, there is nothing of the intensity of mystic states which can answer for the horror of the immediate world. If Jewish wit is permeated, as Theodore Reik believes, by the Biblical injunction that "He that shall humble himself, shall be exalted,"[15] then it must be said that Morris is never exalted in his own mind nor in Frankie's. What deciphers the characters' success is their striving, their moral striving, and not some blissful attainment of New Being. Nor is there revelation or contact with transcendent identity. The goal of *The Natural*, that ritual rebirth which would have heralded a brave new world, is utterly closed to Morris and to Frankie; their "victories" change nothing but the heart of the reader. At the most there is, in Martin Buber's famous depiction of the holy men of Chassidism, the "hallowing of the everyday."[16] However, it is a holiness maintained only by endless pain—a tortured merging of the ideal with the real that man sustains without external support.

Indeed, if God exists anywhere in *The Assistant,* He is in Morris Bober's soul. That is why finally Frankie's conversion, like Morris' identity, is clearly a humanistic rather than a religious mystery—though the two are not necessarily exclusive. That is also why the pressure to read the novel in terms of close Judaic allegory is less rewarding than deflecting. Even the question of Jewishness, or a Jewish heart, is less to the point than might be imagined. Jewish tradition shapes the symbolic form of Frankie's conversion, and it animates the novel's central drama; but, in reality, the author would have the reader understand that Morris' saintliness stems from the same sources as Frankie Alpine's worship of St. Francis. When Morris explains to his assistant what a Jew believes, Frankie replies: "I think other religions have those ideas too" (124). Throughout the novel, the young Italian's conversion to Judaism is indistinguishable from his conversion to the saint of Catholicism.[17] If he is circumcised in the final paragraph, he is St. Francis "dancing out of the woods" in the penultimate one.

What lies then at the heart of *The Assistant* is a ritual composed of fragments of myth, Catholicism, and Judaic thought—all pressed into the service of the author's "mystical" humanism. In the final chapter of the novel, all three traditions curiously blend together in a foreshortened cycle which recapitulates all of Frankie's history in the story and decisively reorders it. An entire year—from spring to spring—surrounds the events of the epilogue that begins with the death of Morris, and within this frame the seasons also reassert themselves in the ancient ritual of rebirth. Though Morris dies in the spring, he reappears in the form of the son become the father. Taking over the store completely, Frankie struggles against the lingering claims of the "old self." At times he succumbs, but finally he reasserts the truth of his transformation: "I am not the same guy I was" (234).

If anything, Frankie's isolation as symbolic father is more complete than it had been before. Ida, sitting in her living room, rarely descends the stairs; and Helen is locked for long months in the terror of her indecision, wanting "to be a virgin again and at the same time a mother" (234). In Frankie, she persists in seeing the source of her own failure. To his confession that he had robbed Morris, a confession that in a sense completes his obligation to his past, she can only return passionate denunciation. "Those books you once gave me to read," Frankie retorts, "did you understand them yourself?" (234).

But the weight of Frankie's presence, as well as the awareness that he had kept Ida and Helen alive, in time alters Helen. One day "It came to her that he had changed . . . there could be an end to the bad and a beginning of the good" (243). Though Helen never manages to voice her changing attitude to the Italian grocer, she does not have to; for Frankie completes through his own efforts the transition of romantic, egotistic love into nutritive love. Reborn and re-integrated, Frankie bears without shame (and in the form of a reddish beard) the emblem of his impurities. Not only the father, he becomes the new lover, the lover for whom the "other" exists not as an extension of his ego, but as a unique being for whom he is responsible. In a sense, in Frankie's final commitment, in his efforts to send Helen to college (and so perhaps out of his life), he emerges from the solipsism which Roy Hobbes could never escape.

For the brief remainder of the novel, there is only, as there was for Morris, the harrowing as well as the "hallowing of the everyday:" the daily ritual of pain and labor and service. And in the spring there is consummation: "One day in April Frankie went to the hospital and had himself circumcised" (246).

VII *Ambiguous Affirmation*

Frankie Alpine's final conversion, of course, carries Malamud directly into the East European and particularly into the Russian tradition of redemptive suffering. If not precisely alien, this concept is at least a mode of affirmation extremely rare in American literary tradition, though perhaps not so rare now that the old affirmative modes posed both by isolation and a return to nature have run into a universal urban reality. But it must be said that even within the Eastern mystical tradition which Malamud celebrates—a mysticism which depends on human relationships —there is still a certain inconclusiveness about the final portrait of Frankie. Rather than representing a new state of being, the grocer's assumption of fatherhood represents a painful integration. As Malamud writes, the circumcision both "enraged and inspired him" (246); but in no way does it alter the ambiguity of his role or the reader's sense of an only partial success. Indeed, for many readers the conclusion of *The Assistant* is the most puzzling section of the entire novel. For Jew *and* Christian, the conversion often seems neither Jewish nor Christian; but, instead, it is incomplete and grotesque. Such criticisms, however, seem to stem from the reader's traditional expectations. For all his patterned ascension to sainthood, the final stages of Frankie Alpine's career, unlike Raskolnikov's, *are* inconclusive and weak. But both qualities, far from robbing the book of its power, are central to its over-all intent and, more, to its over-all persuasiveness.

To comprehend the conclusion, one must understand both the nature of Malamud's themes and the art by which he liberates them. In large part, the final stages of Frankie's history reflect what Malamud had said at the Princeton Symposium, when he maintained that the direction of the novel of the future lies in a fusion of realism and symbolism, or better, in the "more than realistic."[18] What seems clear about Malamud—or at least as clear as such an ambivalent state can allow—is that he is a pessimist who *believes*. From the realists, or at least from his own contact with the world, he has derived a full measure of despair, of the futility of human values in the face of contemporary reality. The avenues of romantic redemption—nature, romantic love, power, individuality—are all echoed in his work; and all are painfully discounted. Like so many of his contemporaries, Malamud sadly delights in picturing those reversals which call traditional values into doubt or in portraying the self in battle with an amorphous public world that turns the self into an absurd posturing Quixoticism. But at the same time, and even if it appears paradoxical, Malamud is also an affirmative writer. He believes in the mystery of the human personality and its power to remake itself, even in the face of the "laws" of history and science. Like F. Scott Fitzgerald, he apparently holds two opposed ideas in balance; and, as with the earlier writer, for Malamud the conflict is dramatic gain.

The force of this tension, mirrored in the conflict of technique, is of course expressible only in irony; and nowhere in *The Assistant* is that irony so clear as in the conclusion. The final paragraph which recounts Frankie's conversion and circumcision is underscored by a tone so flat, is so clearly an anti-climax, that the affirmation is immediately in doubt. Moreover, the circumcision itself can be read, as Ihab Hassan suggests, as an act "of symbolic castration."[19] Indeed, Helen's cry—"Dog—uncircumcised dog!"—echoes to the last moment of the novel; and it has its share, a large one, in mitigating the affirmation. In short, although Frankie Alpine is the hero of saintly redemption—the son who manages to say "yes" to life by saying "no" to self—his success is woven through with the texture of defeat. The poverty remains, the store remains, and with them remains also the obverse side of transcendence: the psychological echoes of something less than saintliness, perhaps a good deal less.

The impurity of the conclusion of *The Assistant*, however, is nothing new in Malamud, nor for that matter in modern literature. What is crucial for Malamud, as for so many writers currently adrift in a sea of fragmented values, is not so much *being* as becoming, not so much conclusions as possibilities. Almost all of Malamud's major works end inconclusively, and almost all of them point to a future in which the struggle is not arrested but in a sense is only beginning. But such conclusions are only the artistic response to what has been the author's special burden from the beginning of his career: to find a form which can resolve belief and doubt in a single instance.

What, in fact, is primarily convincing about his affirmation is its doubtfulness—a paradox that also harks back to the author's Chassidic inclinations. As Martin Buber observes in his study of that order and its dedication to what he calls "holy insecurity," "faith must encompass not expunge doubt."[20] The paradox also explains the nature of Frankie's ridiculous claim to Helen: "Even when I am bad I am good" (140). In the conclusion of *The Assistant*, and for that matter throughout the novel, it is precisely this curious tension which turns the work into an original document. Neither realistic nor symbolic, neither old-fashioned nor modern, it seems to be a synthesis of many tongues; and each, with its traditional burden of theme, has been pressed into service to liberate a distinctive vision: to elaborate the mystery of personality as Malamud understands it and to analyze the forces of inhumanity which he profoundly respects.

VIII *Theme and Technique*

It is precisely because of the impurities of Malamud's method that attempts to classify *The Assistant* as realistic or symbolic always seem to encounter an opposing vein. The very structure and style of the work are ambivalent and are riddled by the same paradoxes that motivate the theme. If the setting in its drab evocation is reminiscent of the social tracts of the 1930's, there is always the persistent feeling that the Bober store is on the point of fading away. And if, in its unremitting sense of defeated character, the novel reminds us of the Dreiserian mode, the "realism" is suffused not only with psychological acuteness but with an equally persistent if enigmatic sense of the Dostoevskian mysteries that enlarge human potential. In fact, although Malamud maintains his omniscience carefully (though not too carefully), the pattern of *The Assistant* is powerfully supported by dream vision. In the intensity of suffering, each character moves in a world which, though substantial, threatens at any moment to turn spectral. Perhaps the best instance of this method is Morris Bober's confrontation with his "other," the red-haired *macher*; but equally impressive is the manner in which the author has suggested, either by key action or key discourse, the way in which all the characters complement or oppose one another in the form of doubles. Inviolable in their immoral separateness, there is yet the constant impression that the characters are in reality a single fractured consciousness. Karp and Morris, Frankie and Ward, all seem to whirl together into a single confused entity.

The "world" of *The Assistant* is, therefore, strangely unstable. From first to last it is dominated by ironic appearances and by strange wayward lines and figures that illuminate the Bober store at the same time that they darken it. Breitbart, the peddler of light; Al Marcus, the paper-bag salesman; the old Polish lady who comes daily for her three-cent roll—they are like ghosts weaving together the moral texture of the story. When they speak—which they rarely do—their voices have little relevance to the universe of defeat they inhabit. When Al Marcus, stricken by cancer, explains to Frankie why be goes on laboring, he says: "If I stay home, somebody in a high hat is gonna walk up the stairs and put a knock on my door. This way let him at least move his bony ass around and try and find me" (87). Insubstantial as air, these old refugees charge the narrative with possibility.

Malamud's skill in investing tangibility to these spectres by re-creating their special idiom has been noted by many critics. But more than skilled mimicry is involved. The Yiddish idiom, with its dedication to ironic understatement in the face of evil, and withal its tendency to deflect pain into gentle paradox, is clearly an aspect of Malamud's theme. "What kind of winter can be in April?" asks Morris on the final day of his life. And that night, speaking with Helen, Morris reveals love, guilt, and saintliness in a few lines of dialogue. Curiously, Helen too, in her moments of direct emotion, speaks the same "language."

> "I remember when you were a little baby," Morris said.
> She kissed his hand.
> "I want the most you should be happy."
> "I will be." Her eyes grew wet. "If you only knew all the good things I'd like to give you, papa."
> "You gave me."
> "I'll give you better." (224)

And even Frankie is blessed with two tongues. In one chapter he can commit a near rape; in the next he can say: "My heart is sorrowful" (184). The ambivalence which marks the assistant is, therefore, a central aspect of his voice. Perhaps the best revelation of this characteristic is the author's recounting of Frankie's hunger for Helen—a recounting that sounds like a modified version of the Song of Songs: "Flower-like panties and restless brassieres . . . breasts like small birds in flight. . . . ass like a flower" (60, 75).

The omniscience of the narrator, in other words, is deceptive, for his sensibility intervenes repeatedly. When Morris and Breitbart weep together over the sorrows of the past, or when Frankie dons his apron, the descriptions clearly convey the sense of ritual and ritual contact. At times, in fact, the Yiddish idiom becomes one with the narration itself, as in this early section describing Morris' history in the store: "In twenty-one years the store had changed little. Twice he had painted all over, once added new shelving. The old-fashioned double windows at the front a carpenter had made into a large single one" (4-5). Even if not idiomatic for the most part, the style swings constantly between the countering claims of ironic understatement and lyricism, harshness and softness; or it fuses together into what Baumbach has called a "gnarled poetry."[21] But it is, in effect, the poetry of the actual and the possible.

The wonder is, of course, that the "technical" debate works; for, by virtue of its working, *The Assistant* not only represents a successful experiment in the "philosophy of the possible," but manages this success by virtue of creating a new or at least a radical form of the novel. In its curious blend of techniques, the work reflects, perhaps self-consciously, the same understanding that recently prompted Saul Bellow to write that "modern writers sin when they suppose that they *know,* as they conceive that physics *knows* or that history *knows.*" And he adds: "The subject of the novelist is not knowable in any such way. The mystery increases, it does not grow less as types of literature wear out. It is, however, Symbolism and Realism or Sensibility wearing out, and not the mystery of mankind."[22]

Bellow's statement might very well serve as an epigraph to Malamud's entire body of work, as well as an indication of his signal success in *The Assistant*. As a novelist, Malamud's struggle is curiously like Frankie's own moral struggle—an effort to escape contemporary limitations and rejoin the prophetic vision of the past—a vision which, as Richard Sewell observes in his study of tragedy, is constant but is only kept alive by forging a new form.[23] Against the appalling forces of the world, which no man of imagination can deny, Malamud has pitted both his love and belief. The result is a world too corrosive and bitter to be anything but true; but it is also a world charged with elusive "holiness," a precarious sense of human potential. Though one cannot read the book without a sense of horror, one cannot read it without a sense of hope. Though it is not quite a record of defeat, it is not quite a record of redemption. In any case, the book has brought to literature something long absent: a sense of awe both for man's capacity to endure and for his enigmatic powers to create himself anew.

CHAPTER *4*

A New Life

"But college was not the synagogue . . ."[1]

BERNARD MALAMUD

SINCE THE PUBLICATION of *The Assistant* in 1957, Bernard Malamud's position in American letters has been secure. If the dark agonies the book recorded elicited dismay from a few critics (to be balanced by others who rejected its pieties), none denied its power. Called a masterpiece by many early reviewers, it has in the intervening years consistently held a high and often central position in most discussions of contemporary fiction. In fact, not a few critics persist in investing this slim work with the prophetic weight of their hopes for some radical departure in the novel.

But despite such acclamation, which has by now become international, it is also true that *The Assistant* has inspired, and continues to inspire, a small body of criticism; and if not particularly intense, it is particularly repetitious. Alfred Kazin was perhaps the first to strike the note when he complained in an early review of the attenuated realism in the novel, of what he described as the author's "natural taste for abstraction."[2] More recently, Philip Roth called attention to the same problem and pressed it to a final conclusion. Commenting on the spectral quality of *The Assistant* and many of the short stories, Roth concluded that Malamud "does not—or has not yet—found the contemporary scene a proper backdrop for his tales of heartlessness and heartache, of suffering and regeneration." To liberate his affirmative vision, Roth suggested, Malamud had to create a world.[3]

I *Function of the Setting*

Behind such criticism there is, of course, a peculiarly demanding view of literature. But what is so instructive about Roth's attitude is that Malamud himself seems to concur. In 1961, five years after *The Assistant,* he published *A New Life;* and the novel (as well as the short stories which have appeared since then) indicates that Malamud considered this work an attempt to amalgamate and complete the drift toward a more realistic fiction that marked the transition from his first to his second novel. Not only is *A New Life* Malamud's largest and freest work, an unpredictable picaresque as openly unrestrained as the *The Assistant* was restrained, but it is also, as one critic put it, "one of the few novels not journalism, of the mid-century, that contains specific speculations on Korea, the cold war, McCarthyism, Hiss and Chambers, loyalty oaths, the plight of liberalism, the definition and the duties of radicalism."[4] The time which frames *A New Life* is the early 1950's, the period in which "the cold war blew on the world like an approaching glacier. . . . and Senator McCarthy held in his hairy fist everyman's name."[5] But what is most important is that the author's depiction of the world of *A New Life* demonstrates conclusively that the time is *actually* the 1950's and that the setting of *A New Life,* a sprawling college town in a Northwestern state, is a real one.

If only for this reason, *A New Life* represents something of a "new" Malamud, or at least a Malamud who rejects the "mythic placelessness" of *The Natural* and *The Assistant* in order to find a more persuasive frame by which to demonstrate his theme of "suffering and regeneration." As the author himself said while composing the work, he intended *A New Life* to be a novel after the manner of Stendhal;[6] and, despite the difference in circumstances, he has to some degree succeeded. In the history of S. Levin, the past-drenched instructor and hero of *A New Life* who seeks a rebirth in the corrupt society of Cascadia College, Malamud has caught, if not the particulars, at least the spirit which animated Stendhal's depiction of Paris during the Bourbon Restoration.[7] What is more, Malamud has caught this atmosphere on almost every level.

Where the "spirit" is most evident, however, is in the thoroughness with which Malamud describes the world of Cascadia

College and, in particular, its English Department, the true antagonist in the story. If in essence the portrait offers nothing particularly new to academic literature, it does in sum.

One of those land-grant "people's institutions" neither old enough for tradition nor young enough to change, Cascadia is frankly awful, and the English Department is the worst thing about it. Ruled by an aged and temperate chairman, Orville Fairchild, its entire orientation has been for decades the preservation of a comatose status quo, and its pride is not the humanities but rather "wholesome snappy drill" in the *Elements of Grammar*. As Levin is informed on his arrival in Eastchester, the College had lost the humanities shortly before World War I and never regained them.

That Cascadia is victimized both by a succession of "false" fathers and by the general pressures of the illiberal, anti-human forces afoot in the land is the prime burden of Malamud's analysis. To S. Levin's compound of appetites, particularly his appetite for the "liberal arts which feed our hearts" (28), the College offers only the sleepy satisfactions of the "good life." And to demonstrate this fact, almost half the novel is devoted to a full, unsparing catalogue of characters, almost all of them emotionally crippled or out of touch with self, and to an equally clinical investigation of the sources of fear and exhaustion endemic to faculty parties and departmental politics.

II S. *Levin*

Much of the analysis, needless to say, is funny. But the distinctive humor lies less in the portrait of the school than in the collision of the College with S. Levin, a former drunkard and inveterate romantic, who brings to the Edenic but rainy clime a hunger for life at its most intense and most fulfilling. Dressed in a solemn black suit and a stiff, black fedora, and carrying an umbrella against the rain, Levin enters Cascadia not only as an Eastern alien but as a disturbing figment from a more moral but nonetheless terrifying past. Half threat and half joke, Levin elicits from Cascadia's plaid-shirted and easygoing inhabitants both laughter and uneasy hostility. In the end, he must be exorcised.

If half of Levin's time in Cascadia, however, becomes the

agency for eliciting the corruption of the place, the other half—
and the more distinctively Malamudian half—belongs to a reverse encounter: the role of Cascadia in eliciting the corruption
in Levin. However refracted by circumstances, thirty-year-old
Levin with his Master's degree is still a refugee from the tenements. Trailing melancholy clouds from the Diaspora, Levin may
hide behind the beard which he grew because he couldn't stand
the sight of his face; but on numerous occasions one finds not
only Frankie Alpine but Morris Bober himself peeking out of
the hairy shadows.

Indeed, the most interesting facet of *A New Life* is that it
represents precisely Malamud's attempt to find a new vehicle
for his distinctive drama, to test his ritual themes against the
recalcitrance of contemporary reality. Although the nature of
Levin's enlarged appetites may obscure the fact, his experiences
in nature, in teaching, in departmental elections, and most distinctively in love affairs sound with a new completeness the ritual
of redemption that has always been the author's primary concern.
An underground man yearning for a new life (a phrase which
Frankie Alpine coined), Levin is a humanist; but he is also a
man of principles out of touch with his principles. He is the
lineal descendent of the prophets but also the orphaned son
of a crook. With a name as procrustean as his various identities
("S," "Sy," "Seymour," "Lev," "Sam"), Levin is the same tortured
image of the unintegrated man met in the earlier works.

What has brought S. Levin to the West, in fact, and what in
turn keeps him bounding from values to values, is the same
determining past which brought Frankie Alpine to rest in the
Bober store. As Levin later reveals in his confession to Pauline
Gilley—the author's latest version of Iris Lemon—the death of a
love affair and the suicide of a hysterical mother had thrust
him out of life into a crawling basement where for two years
he had existed in a drunken stupor. But one morning, awakening
dully, the sight of the sunlight striking his shoes had evoked a
spiritual "turning": "I came to believe what I had often wanted
to, that life is holy. I then became a man of principles" (201).

Levin's morality, moreover, is precisely the agency of the
dark, comic despair which attends his efforts to win joy, success,
and freedom in the larger world. Though little is overtly made
of his Jewishness, the omissions are deceptive. Like Morris the

shlemihl, the sad-faced Levin is a man who "creates his own peril" (58); and for his ceaseless yearning to connect with life, and particularly a life of romantic values, he must suffer the indignity of abrupt reversals. At times, his suffering may be no more than a wrestling in dreams with an "older" Levin who is determined that the instructor shall not forget him. Most often, however, the older self refuses to abide either within the boundaries of a dream or behind a beard. Like a vindictive ghost, the unacknowledged Levin, like the unacknowledged Bober, persists in undercutting each apparent success whether in nature, in sexual experiences, in friendships, or in scholarship. Indeed, he is the prime agent in keeping Levin, though he yearns for dignity, a clear-cut instance of the unadaptive clown who, afire with the need to uplift his students, conducts his first lecture with his fly unzipped. Similarly, each of Levin's attempts to find satisfaction in the larger world that Cascadia College represents ends with equally abrupt calamities. Like Morris Bober, Levin is his own crucial enemy.

In saying as much, however, one quickly recognizes that in some ways S. Levin represents a decisive "enlargement" of the old grocer and his assistant—for neither Frankie nor Morris could survive in Cascadia College for a moment. Malamud's major task in creating his hero was, in fact, to preserve the ritual of rebirth proper to *The Assistant* but to make it operate in dual roles. As several critics have noted, *A New Life* is really two books. On the one hand an academic satire, it traces Levin's history in Cascadia from the August day he arrives to the morning in June when he leaves with wife and children. On the other hand the book is a love story which, while unusually romantic, places demands on Levin that are highly reminiscent of Frankie's love for Helen.

What holds the two levels of the novel in balance is a sudden extension of theme. Malamud seems in part to be arguing that the rebirth of a humanist depends upon many of the spiritual resources that attended Frankie Alpine's birth as a Jew; and to illustrate this point, the author imports into the cycles of Levin's affairs at school and in love certain strategic parallels. As the mythic ritual demands a symbolic ascension of lover into father, Levin, on first meeting Pauline Gilley, must listen uneasily to her enthusiastic account of the virtues of her now dead bearded father. Similarly, in his first interview with Chairman Fairchild, Levin finds himself equated with Fairchild's dead father, a drunkard who had worn "whiskers remarkably like yours and had your color brown eyes. . . . One thinks of the Hebrew patriarchs and the prophets" (50). Throughout the novel, S. Levin's retreat from love is matched by a retreat from ideals; and his failures in both areas stem from the same source.

What gives dramatic unity (uneasy at best) to the thematic complexity is Levin himself. If Levin is a Jew, he is also a dreamy-eyed idealist—an underground man yearning to come above ground to find connection with whatever the world may promise of a better life. Ultimately, Levin must renounce these promises and renounce them precisely because he *is* a Jew first and a dreamy-eyed idealist second. In truth, Malamud suggests at several points that the values the instructor seeks in the West had been invented by him to take the place of the wisdom he has allowed to "drift out" of his consciousness (202). But what has drifted out of Levin's consciousness, but not out of his dreams, is the certain knowledge that the values he seeks are doomed in the real world.

The author's desire to enlarge the patterns of ritual development which motivated the earlier heroes, and yet allow these patterns to operate in the world he describes in *A New Life*, has presented the most difficult problem of characterization. Curiously enough, Levin differs most markedly from such characters as Frankie Alpine or Morris Bober neither in his intellect nor in his ideals (disappointingly, it is impossible to believe in either), but rather in the energy with which he seeks a connection with his world. In most respects, S. Levin is surely the most intense of Malamud's heroes. At times he seems to be nothing so much as a man in the process of lifting both himself and his world by his own emotional bootstraps. In contrast to the weary Morris and the disconsolate Frankie, Levin hungers for Truth, for Beauty, and for Love as Roy Hobbes hungered for food. Indeed, Levin's resources of spiritual *élan* are so profound that it is often impossible to believe him sane.

Where Levin's emotional enlargement over the earlier heroes is clearest can be seen by comparing his attempts to realize himself outside the ritual demands imposed upon him with Frankie Alpine's similar attempts. When Levin, for instance, desires sexual fulfillment, his yearning never takes the form of a peeping-tom. Instead, he sees himself as a lover extraordinary who rides from one conquest to another. At other times (such fulfillment inevitably denied), he succumbs with "sizzling armpits" to the projected image of Professor Levin, the humanist with a big stick who is creating a renaissance in Cascadia's joyless wastes. And when both love and humanities are denied (also inevitably the case), he too seeks fulfillment in the world of nature—but never by simply entering a park.

By virtue of its blooming environs and rain-drenched fertility, Cascadia College offers Malamud his fullest opportunity to investigate the romantic longing for integration in the life of nature. Indeed, a good part of *A New Life* is simply a mock pastoral in which S. Levin, clearly modeled after the Levin of *Anna Karénina*,[8] seeks a Rousseauistic elevation—a return not just to pioneer promise but to the expansive image of nature which supported it. But while each encounter with Cascadia's vegetative largess wrenches from Levin a cry of exaltation, he ultimately suffers reproof. For asking more of nature than it can give a New York Jew (on the final page Levin reflects that a beautiful country is fine if "beauty isn't all that happens" [366]), he must listen to gigantic salmon cry in dreams "Levin, go home" (24) and find that in pastures his feet unerringly carry him into brambles and cow-pies. From each encounter with the emblems of the pioneer life, Levin returns to his tiny room to play host to wave after wave of despair. But so intense are his agonies that they are difficult to distinguish from his ecstasies.

As we will see in the study of *The Magic Barrel*, Malamud's creation of a "levitating Levin" might well have been anticipated from the short stories. But the purposes served by the creation of such a character, who is in truth the "sop of feeling" and "luftmensch" that Malamud calls him, are varied. For one thing, Levin's enthusiasms dramatically counterpoint the rhythm of his conclusion when the promise of a new life is blighted and he assumes the life of patience and submission. For another, his emotional excesses, all motivated by a yearning to find a place for his ideals in the real world, identify the comic hero: the picaresque saint who, Quixote-like, seeks to overwhelm the evils of the world with enthusiasm. Levin's harebrained ecstasies and agonies may make us doubt his sanity, but they also lend an absurd grandeur to his foibles. But most importantly, Levin's emotions plainly represent a dramatic strategy on the part of the author. Through them, he has himself managed to overwhelm the rigidities of the world he describes and keep alive the ambiguous relationship of character and environment of *The Assistant*. Before the force of Levin's passion even the materials of *A New Life*, no matter what their solidity, often seem on the point of disappearing.

III   *Structure and Character*

Levin's intensities have also one further role to play in the novel; for, through them, or at least through the record of their peaks and valleys, the reader is able to keep track of the ritual progression of his life in the West. Though rich in incident (the plot of *A New Life* is plainly too complex to be produced in full), the novel ultimately falls into two almost equal sections corresponding to the changes in the seasons and to Levin's serial struggles with Cascadia and with self. The earlier section, from fall to winter, carries the instructor through a score of disappointments with false fathers, corrupt associates, despondent classes and plagiarizing students; and it ends finally with Levin in retreat from failure in all areas. Indeed, it ends with the contemplation of suicide. The second section, which begins at this point, involves Levin in a love affair with Pauline Gilley, a political crisis in the Department of English, and his subsequent rebirth and dismissal from the school.

By all odds the first section, from the point of technique, is the more interesting. Substantially a record of anticipations blighted, it is principally concerned with Levin's encounters with false images. Yearning for direction, Levin seeks to drown the memory of his interview with Fairchild by finding others who might supply a guideline for entry into the world; and the search is Malamud's opportunity to present a gallery of types ranging from the preposterous to the banal, but never quite to the human.

Perhaps the most interesting of the lot is C. D. Fabrikant, the "liberal" department scholar and gentleman farmer who appears to the instructor's authority-starved eyes like U. S. Grant.

C. D., however, is hardly the father Levin seeks. Instead he ultimately proves to be only another of Levin's false Levins—an unmarried anti-feminist whose liberalism is viable only by virtue of his closed office door behind which he pursues such causes as the correction of "indiscriminate garbage dumping and dogs that run loose and murder his chickens" (232).

If Levin cannot find a father on the Cascadia staff, neither can he find a companion. He "wanted friendship and got friendliness; he wanted steak and they offered spam" (125). With few exceptions his colleagues are either victimized by fear of their positions or their identities swim in a sea of indeterminacy. Levin's isolation is so complete, in fact, that the friendliest of his colleagues, Gerald Gilley, director of composition, is his profoundest enemy; and the only person he can identify with, Leo Duffy, never makes an actual appearance in the novel. In truth, Duffy had committed suicide long before Levin arrived at the college.

It is, however, precisely these characters who dramatically support Levin's dilemma. Though he lives in Gilley's former rooms, he works in Duffy's former office; and with notable anxiety he finds himself bounding first to Gilley and then, on the rebound, to Duffy, as he ferrets out like a self-hypnotized detective the facts of Duffy's career. Together, Gilley and the public memories of the dead Duffy decipher not only the primary paths Levin can choose at Cascadia, but the destruction involved in both.

The doom posed by Gilley is reminiscent of the "false way" of the earlier novels. A fanatic hunter-fisherman-photographer, a wreaker of havoc in the woods, Dr. Gilley is also the prime apologist for the good life, for grammar instead of humanities, for comfort instead of ecstasy. An exemplar of the "reverse hero" (in addition to being red-haired, Gilley is also "seedless," his children adopted), it is Gilley who first names Levin "Sy" and so establishes him, Theodore Solotaroff notes, as the "solemn faculty screwball and radical *naif*"[9] who represents not a challenge to Gilley's future ascendancy to the chairmanship, for which he will contend with C. D. Fabrikant, but instead a colorful instrument of support. Fearful of endangering his career, Levin becomes "Sy"; and he succumbs with only a murmur to the discovery, imparted by Gilley, that he will teach only composition courses. "Nice people," Levin thinks in desperation.

To the extent that Levin retreats from Gilley (the ideal-shattering way to a safe life), he finds himself in "self-love" drawn to Duffy (325). Although he can never quite voice the grounds of his involvement with the radical Irishman, the pertinacity with which he tracks down the history of the liberal man of standards is itself sufficient commentary on his motivations. Throughout the novel, in fact, Levin's encounters with the memory of the big-jawed Irishman from the East (Chicago) who had aroused the hatred of Gilley and been publicly discharged from the school, sound like Frankie Alpine's relationship to Morris Bober—a contact at once a collision and an embrace. While the full story of his predecessor's life at Cascadia remains hidden to the end (when Levin discovers he had been fired on evidence of an affair with Gilley's wife), the image of Duffy disgraced and discharged lingers in the hero's mind like a prophecy from the tomb. Daily, Levin vows to eradicate the Duffy within, but for such denial the night brings dreams in which Levin finds himself in furious combat with the Irishman.

Agonies such as these are daily features of Levin's early and late days in Eastchester; and when classes finally begin—the one remaining solace—the glories of teaching prove as empty as everything else. To his exuberant disquisitions on values, the class returns only somnolence and skepticism. In withdrawal, Levin seeks contentment in his room. But loneliness sends him reeling into a search for feminine contact: in reality, though he cannot admit it, into a search for love. Although Levin had awakened in his hole in the ground to a sense of life's holiness, he had not yet awakened to the love which makes those principles an actuality. "The thought of love," as he later puts it in his confession, "was unbearable" (201). In place of love, Levin seeks conquest; and although the bearded moralist has more insight than Frankie ("If I want sex," he says at one point, "I must be prepared to love" [139]), he is still Levin at war with the morality which defines his nature. For denying his real needs, his "success" is undercut by accidents which are, finally, only the eruptions of his denied personality.

The scenes recounting the hero's bouts with lust carry Malamud's humor to the edge and sometimes directly into anti-romantic farce. In an early chapter, Levin finds himself about to make love in a barn to a waitress he had taken from an improbable Syrian graduate student. "In front of the cows," thinks Levin. "Now I belong to the ages." But, just as he is about to have her, the Syrian discovers the love-nest and steals their clothes (80-82). The next time it is with Avis Fliss, the only single woman instructor in the English Department. Avis, however, later revealed as Gilley's stooge and spy, is only another form of Memo Paris, disciple of evil. Locked in his office with her one night, Levin is about to consummate the love-play when the symbolic taint of the false mother materializes. Avis is suffering from a damaged breast, and Levin's passion flows quickly into pity and then into impotency (133). On the third occasion, however, with his student Nadalee Hammer-stand, there is "success"—but only at the expense of the lost legion of ideals that, in passing, turn the scene into a nightmare comedy. For transforming a student into an object of sexual desire, Levin plays host to a guilty fantasy of himself as Oedipus to Nadalee's Hecuba. But desire is irresistible. Mounted in his battered Hudson, Levin, though he can barely drive, motors desperately over the mountains toward a rendezvous by the sea.

The drive, the maddest section of the novel, is an abandoned *tour de force* in which the lustful *picaro* does battle with the amorphous forms of himself: a little man like Chaplin (in a car with a Eastern license plate) who almost forces him off the road; an impenetrable fog ("Where is the fog, in or out?"); a mysterious old man who gives wrong directions; and a log that looms like a phallus big enough to threaten mankind. But Levin, rescued by an old farmer with a toothache, finally stumbles exhaustedly into Nadalee's arms. Like all of Levin's struggles for romantic fulfillment, however, the affair immediately turns rank. What had started as Levin's rendition of Poe's "Annabel Lee" turns into a Marx Brothers travesty. A few days later, Nadalee "looked like no one he particularly knew" (142-51, 159).

IV *Pauline Gilley*

Levin's moral revulsion over his loveless affair with Nadalee coincides with the coming of winter, a miserable cold, and a direct plunge into despair that seals the first half of the novel.

Having touched bottom, Levin begins to contemplate the end of his struggle for ideals: "the sad golden beauty of a fifth of whiskey" (164). But at this point Levin is born anew, and *A New Life* starts its second movement. Bearing lemons and oranges, Pauline Gilley enters the room on a warm and mythic wind. While, to the rise and fall of her sympathetic voice, Levin feigns sleep, his resistance is pretense—an unsuccessful struggle against what he had unconsciously recognized on the day of his arrival at Cascadia: that Pauline was perilously linked to his own destiny. Though he answers her not a word, the visit is his restoration. When Pauline leaves, Levin rises from his sickbed and returns to a world transformed. Instead of winter, he discovers a landscape dripping with light.

Levin's reaction to Pauline echoes strongly the pattern of Roy Hobbes's experiences with Iris Lemon. Although the passion with which Levin yearns for a successful future as a teacher as well as Pauline's obvious limitations (she is not only married but neurotic and flat-chested) make him reject her, the unconscious dawning of love rebounds into his job. From Pauline's visit, Levin returns to classes discontent over his teaching and intent on reforming himself in his profession.

The affair with Pauline has its real beginning, however, on a "spring" day in January when Levin enters what seems to be an enchanted forest in order to contemplate the flight of birds. Instead, he finds Pauline; and, with a total lack of reflection, they leap upon each other in an act made up of equal parts myth, love, and romantic duplicity. The scene is frankly ironic; for, though the act is surprisingly easy and complete, a "triumph" in the woods, both the setting and Levin's responses are as equivocal as a spring in winter. For one thing, the setting is not the pastoral forest that Levin thought; instead, it is an extension of Cascadia College itself—a training ground for foresters. Moreover, though Levin, in part the old principled lover, the "Lev" that Pauline suddenly calls him, confesses with only minor hesitation the full horror of his past and his shame, he at the same time resists thinking of the future and resists also the compulsion to call Pauline his "love."

Levin's indecisiveness comes to a head in the next few days while he plays gloating host to Pauline in his room and vows "to keep romance apart from convenience" ("love goes with

freedom in my book"). But Levin denied is, of course, Levin
still. For his equation of love with freedom, the "Lev" within
demands retribution. In time the "price of emission becomes a
fiery pain in the ass" (213) which sends the anxious teacher
to a country doctor who mutters, "Beats me . . . unless you
don't like your wife" (215). Damning amateur psychologists,
Levin drives home in the Hudson but can't get the diagnosis out
of his mind. In a moment, as is his way with illuminations, he
begins to levitate: "What was the painful egg the rooster was
trying to lay," he thinks. The answer arrives immediately: "Love
ungiven had caused Levin's pain." With a clatter, he falls in
love (215-16).

So much at least Malamud allows to his hero of the cycle of
redemption through love. In the days after his revelation in the
car, the affair swings into a touchingly rich and tender romance.
Paralleling the dawn of love, Levin's ideals are invigorated and
his courage steeled. By night, he dreams of a domestic life with
Pauline; by day, of a mighty triumph for the forces of liberalism.
One day he even shaves off his beard (self-hatred gone) and
finds that his jaw has grown stronger.

Malamud's description of the love affair fulfills his desire to
write "a romantic love story with warmth and richness."[10] But
at the same time, it is a success which mars the novel. The affair
moves so close to romantic affirmation that the author's real
intent—that "Love is suffering"[11]—can only be salvaged by recourse to an abrupt turnabout. With a suddenness totally un-
prepared for, Levin begins one day to fear for his future and
to doubt Pauline's love. Moreover, Pauline with equal suddenness discovers herself full of guilt and remains frigid through
successive meetings. In the end, when the relationship carries
them close to public discovery, Levin decides to give her up.

The rejection of love is supported by the discovery that
Duffy and Pauline had been lovers. The evidence is a photo-
graph, taken by Gerald Gilley, which shows the two naked on
a beach. Though Levin later denies that it is sufficient evidence
to damn them, it is at the moment sufficient for his unidealistic
purposes. In retreat from the image of Levin as Duffy, he avoids
both the presence and the thought of Pauline in order to find
redemption in his work.

V *The Quest for Fatherhood*

Levin's redemption, however, had begun already; and do what he will, he can only deny, not escape it. If love unbidden began the struggle for ideals in the school, it is love denied that carries Levin into the thick of the battle. Simply, Levin is not the same as before; and the difference is the love he seeks to expiate. Irony is the key; and the irony is persuasive. Although he cannot bear the responsibility for Pauline, he nonetheless seeks responsibility in the department. Not only does he tell Gilley he will not support him for chairman, but he finds he cannot support Fabrikant either. In the end, Levin announces that he himself will run for the post.

The decision, of course, completes the diversion of the myth of the child into the father in a totally new area. At home, giddy with dreams, Levin writes a platform that seems a synthesis of all democratic thought; and in the department, squirming before his colleagues' hatred, he grows incoherent with joy to discover that there are a few who secretly support his candidacy. For a time Levin becomes still another new Levin—the idealist who practices *Realpolitik*—who, like Duffy and his own father, sneaks with moral trembling into Gilley's office to steal evidence by which to defend himself. But, significantly, Levin's incipient success as a politician is undercut as quickly as the love affair with Pauline—and for identical reasons. At the height of his campaign, Pauline returns and Levin, though he longs to reject her, cannot. Agreeing that Gilley be told of the relationship, Levin quickly receives word of his dismissal from the staff.

Levin's failure in the realm of politics, as well as his failure in the realm of romantic love, is again too abrupt to be dramatically convincing. But the difficulty is only in the drama. In reality, Levin is fated to fail from the very beginning, for success in either realm would have meant victory in spite of Levin's own identity and, more importantly, in spite of Malamud's own moral imperatives. In accepting Pauline, no matter her own destructiveness, Levin has in essence accepted himself with all the freight of anxiety that goes with it, including the absolute loss of "the freedom to feel free" (344). He has in fact plunged into a mode of heroism that belongs with *The Assistant*: choosing to leave the way of the *luftmensch* and the liberal dreamer and take the path of submission and suffering.

In some ways, however, Levin's end is even more trying than Frankie's, for his choice is made without the certain knowledge that he is in love with Pauline. Before accepting her, he undergoes a three-day struggle with the totality of his makeshift personality; and always, with crushing indecision, he asks himself where his love has gone. But in truth, love has not gone; it is only transformed into a new and non-romantic form. Though Levin would probably deny he loves Pauline until the last, it is love which allows him to discover "himself by discovering what he is not."[12] Resisting all the inner-voices which speak for escape, for the future, for the realization of all his dreams, love also guides him to his final moment of triumph when, in the finest scene in the novel, the now willing-unwilling father and future husband confronts Gilley to ask for custody of the children. Gilley's reply is a proposition that drives Levin away from any lingering possibility of romantic fulfillment.

In a long peroration, the "false" father informs Levin of what he is getting into by recording with minute detail not only Pauline's emotional instability, her frequent ailments and nervous depressions, but the countless illnesses of the adopted children. "Living with Pauline," Gilley tells him, "is generally no bed of roses." But Levin, his Jewishness, as Frank Kermode noted, suddenly "leaking into the text,"[13] replies: "I have never slept on flowers." Failing to dissuade Levin, Gilley presents a final despairing alternative, one far beyond his own reach. He agrees to give Levin the children on condition that he renounce college teaching. When Levin, his future in final shreds (even Gilley knows that Levin will keep his word), agrees even to this, it is Gilley's turn to wonder: "An older woman than yourself and not dependable, plus two adopted kids, no choice of yours, no job or promise of one, and other assorted headaches. Why take that load on yourself?" Levin's answer, a simple short sentence, plucks him at once out of the determination of the past, present, or future: "Because I can, you son of a bitch" (358-60). This declaration places him in a thin zone of freedom where man confronts manhood in the most painful of acts: the freedom to choose the absence of freedom.

The line, marvelous in its brevity, summarizes Malamud's early and late bouts with man's struggle to rise above himself. With pain and desperation, Levin chooses responsibility and defeat; and the choice represents the upwelling of an ancient morality that is part Hebraic, as in *The Assistant,* and part mythic, as in *The Natural.* In the final pages of the novel, both elements fuse; for soon after his decision, Levin restores the cycle of mythic triumph for which Roy Hobbes had proved unworthy. While Levin still teeters in indecision, lamenting his promise to Gilley, Pauline informs him—delighting in her swelling breasts—that she is two months pregnant. And in the dawn of incipient fatherhood, Levin reclaims her: "Her body," he notes, "smelled like fresh-baked bread, the bread of flowers" (366). A moment later, starting the Hudson that is to carry himself, his future wife, and children, both borrowed and new, out of the West and into the way of a burdensome "old" life, Pauline cries "God bless you, Lev." To which Levin replies, with what must be willful ambiguity, "Sam, they used to call me home" (366).

With Gerald Gilley snapping pictures of them (and so Levin completes Duffy's sad cycle), Levin, the former romantic and luster after LIFE, rides into the triumphant East and into the sacred prison that was all Frankie Alpine knew of victory.

VI   *The Weaknesses of* A New Life

There is no question, therefore, but that *A New Life,* for all the enlargement of its concerns, belongs squarely in the mainstream of Malamud's thought. Success in failure, failure in success—the ritual conclusion of *A New Life* is the same as that of *The Assistant.* But while one cannot question the relevancy of *A New Life* in terms of its place in Malamud's development, there are numerous questions which must be asked about the book's final value. For it seems distressingly clear that if *A New Life* is Malamud's most ambitious novel, it is also his weakest one. Moreover, it is equally clear that the ambitiousness and the weaknesses go hand in hand. Indeed, what rides with S. Levin at the conclusion of the book is not alone the weight of family, failure, and possibility. These he can bear as well as Frankie. But in addition to these, Levin is damned to carry with him all of his past aspirations and ideals—in truth, the world itself in all its exposed and clamorous variety. And this burden he cannot support. Between Malamud's intentions for his new hero and his dramatization of them, there is simply a great gulf.

The weaknesses of *A New Life,* in other words, stem almost consistently from the author's attempts to find a form that can unite the "two books": the academic world and the intensities of the underground world that appear in *The Assistant.* On the whole, he has not succeeded. Perhaps the most glaring example of this failure is the fact that the effort has severely limited the very reality the author has sought. Despite his intent to create a portrait of society in the tradition of Stendhal, Cascadia College is *not* presented realistically. Nor are its inhabitants. If the characters are continually revealed by virtue of Levin's presence, suggesting depths and pains beyond the resources of parody, they are just as consistently obscured by the impetus of satire which is at times brutal and at others merely playful; but in any case the satire arrests development rather than forwards it. After the initial interview, for instance, Chairman Fairchild's role in the novel, until a brief, hilarious death scene, is exhausted; and he emerges finally not a character but a formula for a bad past. And Gerald Gilley, though the author's plans for him *seem* grandiose, never quite overcomes the status of a terrified academic. Though Gilley suggests origins in Alexei Karénin, satire usurps sympathy.

Even Pauline, one of the more realized characters in the novel, never quite comes alive. The pattern of her life suggests motives and pressures richer than any of Malamud's earlier heroines, but her full character is never separated from Levin's point of view. Because of this limitation, Pauline's personality is constantly obscured and can be effectively felt only by recourse to the kind of ritual gestures and slogans that depicted Iris Lemon. If Gilley is no Alexei, Pauline is assuredly no Anna. Indeed, one of the ironies of the novel is that the most realistic and sympathetic of the characters, an insecure instructor who manages to preserve his integrity in the department and to provide for a wife and five children, is only a minor character; that he "comes off" so well, however, is because the ritual of the "other" book in *A New Life* is not imposed on him. For the rest, both the characters as well as their settings are reduced to another academic set piece which, while very funny, is too familiar to be exciting.

But perhaps the worst problem is that small as Cascadia College is, it is still too large to accommodate Malamud's hero and the intention he is to fulfill. One sign of this failing is the author's inability to authenticate Levin's past in his present (Stendhal, of course, found it necessary to begin with Julien's youth.) While Levin inhabits a present ostensibly real, his early years are not sufficiently detailed to be convincing; they remain instead the ritual past of *The Assistant* and *The Natural*. As one critic put it, it is "difficult to believe after the first chapter that S. Levin was once a drunk."[14] In the same fashion, it is difficult to believe in Levin's mystical revelations.

Moreover, if the author's ritual and moral concerns rob the reader of a sense of the character's past, they also deny him a sense of a tangible present. From first to last Levin is too much the lonely melancholic, the ghetto Jew, to persuade us that he is, in addition, a humanist and a teacher involved in the world of ideals. Though Malamud attempts to so persuade us, he really succeeds only in making Levin a childish enthusiast for the liberal view. As Marcus Klein states, the words "democracy, humanism, liberalism (and the liberal arts), radicalism, freedom, art, and intellect . . . are ever and easily at his lips." But "between Levin's ideals and the social facts there is tremendous distance and a total absence of social analysis."[15] Levin's idealism, in fact, seems to be there only to demonstrate his throbbing "Jewish heart."

But what is most painful about the portrait is the *obvious* signs of Malamud's intent for Levin,—his constant wrestling, as Theodore Solotaroff observes, to "hold the two types in the same characterization."[16] Whenever the pattern of Levin's ritual development is obscured, which it often is, the author must pluck the character out of the world and isolate him in his room either to undergo agony or rebirth. And Levin dies and is reborn with such regularity, and frequently over such trivial events, that it is impossible to entertain a consistent attitude toward him. His reversals in sex and in nature become finally only a series of set jokes and contretemps, and in the end his enthusiasms are more farcical than convincing. Indeed, so indiscriminate is Levin's emotionalizing that one suspects that his final decision may be less the effect of choice than simple exhaustion. That so many critics cannot believe Levin is in love with Pauline at the conclusion of the novel is not to be wondered at. It is only by recourse to Malamud's earlier novels that one can be sure of his love.

Simply, Levin is too frail to absorb Cascadia College or the West; and the author's attempts to assuage the fact by the employment of a style as abandoned as anything in *The Natural* only creates a further difficulty. In the first novel, the style was *intended* to usurp the world; in *A New Life* it does precisely the same thing but at the expense of the sense of reality the book demands. One of the main troubles with *A New Life* is that it is too dazzling, that it proliferates one major effect after another. That the purpose of such episodes is to overwhelm the world and heighten our sense of Levin's resources has already been pointed out. But quite the opposite effect is finally achieved. So repetitious are Levin's ecstasies and so inevitable are his defeats that his adventures soon take on a static, fated, and unexciting quality. In any case, Levin's enthusiasms seem inevitably a matter of tricks of style and not the character's own sensibility. Most of the time, the hero seems only a disagreeable wanton.

Of course, such criticism does overlook much of the novel's power; for, if the work lacks integration, it does possess diversity and vigor. In Levin's limited confrontation with nature, his ride over the mountains, and his interview with Fairchild, there is a genuinely effective madness. For that matter, some of the more concentrated sections, particularly the first chapter, are as good as any Malamud has ever done. Moreover, Malamud does manage to make his points. S. Levin's disappointment, his failure to find connnection with the world and with Truth and Beauty, tell us unequivocally how narrow is the way to grace. Like all of Malamud's better work, the sadness of redemption in *A New Life* proceeds from the author's own pessimism: his loss of belief in what the world, even at its best, can offer contemporary man.

Ultimately, *A New Life* fails only when one compares it to *The Assistant*. By that comparison it becomes all too evident that the academic novel represents, as Jonathan Baumbach suggests, the author's "attempt to extend the range of his concerns beyond the impulses of his talent."[17] Malamud's best works are his second novel and his Jewish tales precisely because of the slimness of social reference which allows the author to meld symbol and reality into a ritual form utterly original and harmonious. Against such works as these the frenetic energy and vitality of *A New Life* seem at best shallow. If, in payment for such achievements Malamud must forego (as Philip Roth suggests) the sense of a concrete and identifiable "now," it is after all small pay for such returns.

In any case it is *not* an author's realism which convinces; only his art does that. Within its own limitations, *The Assistant* is too integrated to allow for comparisons. Only hindsight and abstract talk about the novel itself can really discredit its limited social texture. But *A New Life,* because of the very issues raised and the author's own failure to resolve them, invites questions as one reads. And these questions are pertinent to a consideration of the writer's entire career. Though it is perhaps too easy to suggest, *A New Life* seems to define the limits of the author's realism just as *The Natural* defined the limits of his purely symbolic method. Where Malamud achieves his finest expression —where he is in fact like no other contemporary writer—is in some borderland world, small to be sure, but no less powerful for being small. In this world his vision and his talents, as well as his formal limitations, meld in a novel and remarkable manner.

That he has attempted to extend his talents in *A New Life* is of course testimony to the vitality of his art and his honesty. That he has not succeeded in managing it calls us back again to his best work: to *The Assistant* and to those short stories which manage to embody hope and despair, pessimism and belief in a manner so realized that, as Norman Podhoretz states, "they deserve to live forever."[18]

CHAPTER 5

The Stories

> "There are unseen victories all around us. It's a matter of plucking them down."[1]
>
> BERNARD MALAMUD

The Magic Barrel

ONE OF BERNARD MALAMUD'S early short stories, "The First Seven Years," has an opening sentence so arrestingly simple and clumsy that it demands repeating: "Feld, the shoemaker, was annoyed that his helper, Sobel, was so insensitive to his reverie that he wouldn't for a minute cease his fanatic pounding at the other bench."[2] A good many of Malamud's other stories, both later and earlier than "The First Seven Years," begin in a similarly rough-and-ready fashion. Here, for instance, is the opening of "The Mourners": "Kessler, formerly an egg candler, lived alone on social security" (17)—and here the start of "Take Pity": "Davidov, the census-taker, opened the door without knocking, limped into the room and sat wearily down" (85). The beginning of another story, "The Loan," varies the formula only by the position of the name but enlarges the clumsiness with the intrusion of a rhyme: "The sweet, the heady smell of Lieb's white bread drew customers in droves long before the loaves were baked" (183).

Whatever is apparent in these beginnings, drawn from the first collection of Malamud's short stories, *The Magic Barrel*, it is assuredly not their grace. If anything, they seem, for their matter-of-factness as well as for their suggestion of a rough and untutored speaking voice, to belong to a tradition so old that its reappearance is slightly unnerving. The last thing to expect from the modern author is the author himself. But Malamud never seems to fear his own voice, even if it means sounding like an immigrant out of night school translating the prophets, as in the opening of "Angel Levine," the story of an East Side Job:

> Manischevitz, a tailor, in his fifty-first year suffered many reverses and indignities. Previously a man of comfortable means, he overnight lost all he had, when his establishment caught fire and, after a metal container of cleaning fluid exploded, burned to the ground. Although Manischevitz was insured against fire, damage suits by two customers who had been hurt in the flames deprived him of every penny he had collected. At almost the same time, his son, of much promise, was killed in the war, and his daughter, without so much as a word of warning, married a lout and disappeared with him as off the face of the earth. Thereafter Manischevitz was victimized by excrutiating backaches and found himself unable to work even as a presser—the only kind of work available to him—for more than an hour or two daily, because beyond that the pain from standing became maddening. His Fanny, a good wife and mother, who had taken in washing and sewing, began before his eyes to waste away. (43).

Needless to say, it has been a long time since an author could pass off a line like "His Fanny, a good wife and mother," and make it work. It has been an even longer time since an author's own compassion could convince one of the reality of pains so directly evoked. If one of the tests of a successful author is his ability to make convincing what should *not* be convincing, then Malamud has surely passed the test. In reading his better stories, one has the strange sensation of entering a world in which the most complex of realities masquerade with ease in a motley of folk-wisdom and genuine naïveté. Although the subjects are, as in the novels, the thorny ones of spiritual growth and decay, the terrors of alienation and salvation, there is about many of them an echo of a long dead voice intoning directly, "I will tell you now of dragons."

It goes without saying, of course, that the only thing that can sustain such artlessness is art of a very difficult kind; and so it is that, as a writer of short fiction, Malamud seems to have emerged full-grown and mature with his first collection. Published in 1958, the year after his second novel, *The Magic Barrel* not only received the National Book Award, but more importantly it represents, along with *The Assistant*, his major achievement. If assuredly uneven, the thirteen stories in the work contribute to a triumph rarely granted a writer so early in his career. With them he achieved what many writers, and even better ones, must struggle for years to attain: a voice which is distinctively his own.

I *Literary Traditions*

For this very reason, however, it is also difficult to assess the stories. Norman Podhoretz wrote that the tales possess a quality which "very nearly beggars description."[3] And the general critical response to *The Magic Barrel* bears him out. Blending in some indeterminate way both the resources of naturalism and symbolism, a vernacular steeped at one and the same time in the rhythms of European Yiddish storytelling, and a laconic irony reminiscent of Hemingway, the stories have inspired oddly divergent searches after influences. As a short-story writer Malamud has been called a disciple of I. L. Peretz, a Sherwood Anderson and a Chekhov of the East Side, and frequently an amalgamation of all these things. Nor is the obverse side of the coin slow to rise: one often learns that the Jewish elements in the stories are neither essential nor even particularly significant —even from those critics who readily agree that the "Jewish" stories are precisely the best.

But there is no reason to deny the efficacy of the comparative approach. That Malamud has mastered his craft with the aid of "models" is as true of the stories as of the novels. A good many of the pieces, especially the shorter ones, are approximately if not precisely in the tradition of Yiddish folk-realism; and there is about them, in their pained but rarely bitter evocation of suffering and inhumanity, a narrative echo, as Earl Rovit beautifully put it, "of the eternal chant."

But if the intonations are reminiscent of the literature of the Pale, Malamud's handling of form reveals a sensibility "keenly aware," as Rovit adds, of the "formal demands of the short story."[4] Not only do many of the tales, and even the most "Jewish" of them, rely heavily on the technique of epiphany, but they reveal a formal concentration as spare and as devoted to symbolic design as the stories of Chekhov or Joyce. Moreover, there are times when the stories, both in their fusion of poetry and outright horror, as well as the reiterated images of alienation and psychic crippling, sound curiously like Sherwood Anderson's tales of the grotesque.

II *The Stories and the Novels*

But comparison with other authors, by virtue of the extensiveness of the possibilities, is misleading. For Malamud, borrowed technique seems only the means of shoring up and extending a vision that is essentially his own. That is why, perhaps, the novels themselves offer the readiest and the most illuminating approach to the stories. For not only do the shorter pieces recapitulate the central themes of the novels, but they also reflect in their variety and in their unequal value all the pressures that went into the creation of the three longer works. Variously, and sometimes at once, the stories move from the extremes of symbolism to realism; from a deft and conscious use of myth and ritual to a seeming artlessness; from fantasy to naturalism. In each case, the reader finds also the same interrelationship of fictional modes and successes-and-failures which undercut *The Natural, The Assistant,* and *A New Life.*

In the light of the previous chapters, it might be excepted that the finest achievement in the collection would belong to those stories which share most closely the techniques and the vision of *The Assistant.* Such, in fact, is the case. The half-dozen best stories, and preeminently the title story, though reminiscent of the ethical folk tales of Aleichem and Peretz, unfold in a remarkably tough-minded and spare crucible. In each case the major ingredients are the same. The Jewish heroes, most of them elderly, sit behind closed doors (the essential setting) in a twilight tenement world. With their hungers stripped to fundamentals and their bodies shaken by memories of ancient lore, they manage to translate misery into a bemused humanity. In each case, the dramatic conflict, to which all else is subordinant, is between man and assistant, man and enemy, the pursued and the pursuer. The conflict is so intense at times that it breeds angels and *luftmensch, doppelgangers* and ghosts; but finally it breeds a miracle, a moment of painful unmasking which resolves the conflict and often transforms the hero into something more than he was originally.

III   *The Tales of New York Jews*

The initial tale in the collection, "The First Seven Years,"
might illustrate them all; for the opposition and final integration
of Feld, the shoemaker, and Sobel, his assistant, is pure Malamud. The aged Feld is the real center of the story by virtue
of the special moral demands imposed upon him. Like most of
the protagonists in the stories, Feld must choose between alternate values; and the choice, made in terror and suffering, distinguishes finally the shoemaker from the *mensch*.

Like Morris Bober, Feld is in part the victim of his own
goodness. Spinning daydreams out of the February snow, and
agonizing over memories of his youth in a Polish *shtetl*, the
shoemaker has sworn to create for his daughter Miriam a better
life than he has known. But the dream, with true Malamud
irony, redounds not to Feld's glory but feeds the guilt which
tortures his relationship to Sobel, a spectral young-old refugee
who five years before had saved Feld from ruin by becoming
his assistant. Aware without full consciousness that Sobel labored
only for love of Miriam, Feld arranges a date for his daughter
with a young accounting student who is the harbinger of a
better life. For this action, Feld immediately loses his infuriated
assistant and, for his guilt, his own sense of well-being.

A single date convinces Miriam, who had already been won
by Sobel, that the budding accountant is an inveterate ma-
terialist; and when a new assistant proves a thief, Feld in despair
takes to his bed with a damaged heart. Later, driven by a
complex of needs, the old man pushes himself to Sobel's clut-
tered roominghouse and the kind of confrontation which is
Malamud's special province: a meeting in which the denied self
begins, in pity, to leak past one's guard and for a decisive
moment pours forth in a sanctified stream. Listening to Sobel's
tearful declaration of his love, Feld shuttles from exasperation to
a compassion that proves his undoing:

> Watching him, the shoemaker's anger diminished. His teeth
> were on edge with pity for the man, and his eyes grew moist.
> How strange and sad that a refugee, a grown man, bald and
> old with his miseries, who had by the skin of his teeth escaped
> Hitler's incinerators, should fall in love, when he had got to

America, with a girl less than half his age. Day after day, for five years he had sat at his bench, cutting and hammering away, waiting for the girl to become a woman, unable to ease his heart with speech, knowing no protest but desperation. (15)

Though Feld feels a gripping sorrow for his daughter's future, he submits to the relationship and the return of the assistant. But Feld exacts from the now young-looking Sobel the promise that he wait two years before the marriage (and so invokes the mythic cycle of fertility). That is all of the story; but for Feld there is an instant of real though muted triumph, a gesture which, despite the winter night and the continuous poverty for himself and his daughter, stamps the story with a spectral promise of salvation through love. His success is no more perhaps than the ability to walk the whitened street "with a stronger stride," or to hear, without anxiety, the consecrated labor of his assistant, who, himself now the father and provider, sits at his work desk "pounding leather for his love" (15-16).

Despite the brevity of the form, Malamud's ability to evoke a sense of full experience with an odd verbal twist, as in the last line, or to intimate the Biblical parallels of the story, seems to raise behind the actual story a canvas far larger than the described one. But what sustains "The First Seven Years" most effectively is what sustains *The Assistant*, an alteration of techniques which continually shifts the character into a strange borderland world which becomes the emblem of the author's belief in the possibility of a leap beyond determinism. The intensity of Feld's emotion, the fragments of myth, the grotesque beauty of Sobel, and most particularly Malamud's own beautifully clumsy and compassionate voice charge the story not only with the suggestion of human mysteries but human miracles. Here, for example, is the description of Max, the poor accounting student: "He was tall and grotesquely thin, with sharply cut features, particularly a beak-like nose. He was wearing a loose, long slushy overcoat that hung down to his ankles, looking like a rug draped over his bony shoulders, and a soggy, old brown hat, as battered as the shoes he had brought in" (5).

That Max might pluck a magic flute from the folds of his monstrous coat seems only the result of the faith of the teller himself: that weirdly ironic, poetic voice which reminds the reader—by an occasional clumsiness, a halting rhythm, or the folk tale form itself—that what he is relating is more than just art. What finally makes the miracle most believable, however, is that it does not occur. Malamud's tongue is "forked"; for, though it rings at times with the visionary simplicity of a child, it is nonetheless thick with the sour disaffection of a cynic which enforces upon the whole, despite the clear drift toward sentimentality, a drama of pained possibility.

Techniques so delicately balanced, however, can easily become uncoupled and spill over either into outright fantasy or the grotesque. While it is true that Malamud rarely loses control of his Jewish tales, he does occasionally slip. Stories like "The Mourners" or "Angel Levine" illustrate this tendency.

"The Mourners," the second of the tales, recounts an incident in the life of a sixty-five-year-old retired egg candler who seeks to end his days closeted in a wretched little flat at the top of an East Side tenement. But unlike Morris Bober or Feld, the protagonist, Kessler, is frankly a Jewish grotesque: an aged isolato who had long before forsaken wife and children and now, in filthy old age, devours himself in loneliness, speaking to no man and, for his contempt, being shunned by all. For this reason "The Mourners" is assuredly one of the most dismal stories in the collection, overburdened with a sense of futility that is enlarged by Kessler's fanatic resistance to the landlord's efforts to evict him. The weight of despair is so intense, in fact, that the resolution, despite numerous anticipatory clues, offers less relief than a weird shock.

Climbing to Kessler's flat, Gruber, the landlord, agonizes over his guilty conscience even while intent on reaping the financial rewards that Kessler's eviction promises. Once in the room he finds the old man in a state of mourning, "rocking back and forth, his beard dwindled to a shade of itself." Although Kessler is mourning for himself, for his past misdeeds and for his abandoned wife and children, Gruber, "sweating brutally," decides that Kessler is mourning for *him*. In a gesture that plunges him out of the role of landlord and back into Jewish history, Gruber wraps himself in a sheet and drops to the floor as a fellow mourner (25-26). While spectacular and even haunting, the epiphany of "The Mourners" is simply too abrupt and too meaningful to be supported by the two-dimensional characters and the unrelieved weight of horror. It is, finally, *only* the conclusion which remains in the mind, a sudden frozen tableau.

However, it is quite otherwise with "Angel Levine," the fourth fable in the collection and one which, while drenched in fantasy, exercises a bold, unmistakable magic. By virtue of its very extremes, the story also serves as a map for the implicit fantasy of the other tales. Manischevitz, whose tribulations remind one of a latter-day Job, is offered salvation if only he will recognize in the form of a mysterious visitor—a large bonily built Negro named Alexander Levine—a heaven-sent Jewish messenger. But in outrage against what he believes to be the pretensions of the Negro, and, wonderfully, his own naïve inclination to believe, Manischevitz denies Levine. Moreover, he persists in his denial despite the evidence that Levine's mere presence relieves both the former tailor and his wife Fanny of some of their pains. For his disbelief, however, the pains return in greater fury; and Fanny sinks quickly toward death.

And so Manischevitz, with unwilling willingness, sets out in search of the black angel through the streets of Harlem. His feet carry him to such unlikely spots as a Negro synagogue where a Talmudic disquisition is occurring, then to a satanic honky-tonk where Levine, denied the salvation of Manischevitz's trust, is succumbing to Bella, the Circe of the establishment. In the end, Manischevitz does credit Levine as a Jewish divinity; and for this act he experiences a moment of vision in which he sees the Negro mount heavenward on a pair of magnificent wings. Rushing home to the magically recovered Fanny, the tailor whispers the tag-line to a millennium of Jewish encounters with the unexpected forces of humanity: "A wonderful thing, Fanny," he breathes. "Believe me, there are Jews everywhere" (56).

Because of the supporting fantasy, "Angel Levine" is the only one of Malamud's stories to deal explicitly with the religious implications that offer subtle support to many of the other stories, as well as to *The Assistant*. But the difference is only a question of degree, and the story relies on the same kind of formal tension and resolution that directs the drama in most of the author's fiction. Like Feld, Manischevitz is required to acknowledge the divine essence in another, an act which redeems both the truster and the trustee. Because Manischevitz must extend his trust beyond the confines of differing skins, he has only a more difficult burden than most. What Manischevitz must learn, in fact, is the author's theme that Jews are indeed "everywhere"—in Protestants, in Catholics, in Negroes who can intone Chassidic wisdom in synagogues (54). As Norman Podhoretz has suggested of Malamud's characters, "The Jew is humanity seen under the twin aspects of suffering and moral aspiration. Therefore any man who suffers greatly and who longs to be better than he is can be called a Jew."[5]

But if Jewishness generalized into metaphor and construct is Malamud's subject, the Jew particularized is his triumph. This particularization is certainly true of Manischevitz, whose every gesture or intonation reveals not only superficial Jewish aspects—superbly rendered—but the deeper attitudes and postures which have developed through ages of accommodating ethical vision to historical necessity. The Jobian parallel, in other words, is funny; but it is no joke. In Manischevitz's relationship to God, which runs from mild despair to the sense of abandonment, there is only loving reproof, never disbelief. His prayers, in fact, reveal an elemental closeness to God: "'My dear God, sweetheart, did I deserve that this should happen to me? . . . Give Fanny back her health, and to me for myself I shouldn't feel pain in every step. Help now or tomorrow is too late. This I don't have to tell you'" (44).

That Malamud loves his old Jews, and particularly those in whom misery has only induced more kindliness and gentleness, in unquestionable. Moreover, through them he has managed, as Dan Jacobson has suggested, to achieve "What has baffled and defeated greater writers: the capacity to make goodness of the most humble and long suffering kind real, immediate, and attractive."[6]

"Angel Levine" is, however, only one of the better stories of its kind in the collection. It is certainly not the best, and the trouble seems to be that the fantasy is so enlarged in the service of victory that the story lacks the second property which cinches conviction in Malamud's best work. It lacks failure, the sense of continuing despair. However, in two others of the fables, "The Bill" and "The Loan," the blend of the real and the fantastic, of horror and triumph, borders on the miraculous.

"The Bill," structurally the more complex of the two stories, sounds again the problems of trust, of Jewish-Gentile relations, and of imprisonment in a grocery store which marked *The Assistant;* but it does so with an economy and directness that is remarkable. The opening paragraph is a weird blend of cameo realism and symbology that is sharply angular and impressionistic at the same time:

> Though the street was somewhere near a river, it was landlocked and narrow, a crooked row of aged brick tenement buildings. A child throwing a ball straight up saw a bit of pale sky. On the corner, opposite the blackened tenement where Willy Schlegel worked as janitor, stood another like it except that this included the only store on the street—going down five stone steps into the basement, a small, dark delicatessen owned by Mr. and Mrs. F. Panessa, really a hole in the wall. (145)

Though the relationship of the Schlegels and Panessas supplies the tale with its dramatic center, the story proper belongs to Willy; for he observes the progress of the store and broods upon the disconsolate weariness of his life in an East Side wasteland that promises neither escape nor relief. Wandering into the Panessa store one day, Willy finds himself relating to the attentive Panessas the horrors of his barren life; and, as he speaks, he buys item after item. When he cannot pay, Mr. Panessa offers credit, ennobling the act with the thought ". . . because after all what was credit but the fact that people were human beings, and if you were really a human being you gave credit to somebody else and he gave credit to you" (146-47).

But the tale is not about goodness alone, nor in this case even about particular forms of Jewish goodness. Instead, the subject is the depressing one of how, in a world ruled by the ineluctable demands of economics and accidents, even good can turn rank. Or better, it is a story which depicts the manner in which the soul descends into an embittering nightmare when the need to extend goodness is denied. And Willy Schlegel encounters such a nightmare when, after weeks of frantic buying on credit, the Panessas are forced to ask him for payment. Unable to pay, he retreats from the store, nursing an obscure grievance. As the season turns toward winter, Willy spends the nights dreaming of repaying and the days lamenting his inability to do so. In time, the pain of his guilt transforms his sympathy for the aged couple to hatred. In the spring, there is a momentary turning, a flash of redemption that hovers for a moment over the stony streets. Rising from a dream-filled sleep, Willy dashes to a pawnshop, receives ten dollars for his overcoat, and rushes to the Panessas' store.

When he arrives, a hearse is standing before the grocery and two men are carrying a coffin from the house. Told it is the grocer who lies within, Willy plunges into inarticulate despair in which only the author's words can find a grotesque glory: "He tried to say something but his tongue hung in his mouth like a dead fruit on a tree, and his heart was a black-painted window." The following paragraph, the last, belongs only to the narrator, who is now in full retreat; and it closes out the story with granitic objectivity: "Mrs. Panessa moved away to live first with one stone-faced daughter, then with the other. And the bill was never paid" (153).

Though only eight pages long, the impact of "The Bill" is unaccountably powerful. One senses in it the impersonal weight of a naturalistic universe that balances precariously on the moral give-and-take of a few struggling nonentities—and then quickly crushes them. And in the second of the two stories, "The Loan," the method and the intent are similar—a swift fragment of action that freezes despair into permanent ice and yet leaves within, like Willy's "black-painted window" of a heart, a forlorn and foolish flicker of hope.

Fantasy supports "The Loan," but only as an undercurrent; for the aptly named baker, Lieb, blinded by cataracts and grey with sorrows, is also the dispenser of a strange communion. Though his pastries do not sell, his bread, after thirty years of failure, now "brought customers in from everywhere." The yeast was tears, the misery he wept into the dough. Successful but ill, Lieb tends the ovens while his second wife Bessie serves customers and worries over finances. It is Bessie who first notices the arrival of Lieb's skeletal friend Kobotsky entering the store with a face that "glittered with misery" to greet Lieb after a separation of fifteen years (181).

Overjoyed by the reunion, Lieb seats the grim Kobotsky on a tall stool in the back room, and forgetting the misunderstanding

over a debt that had long ago ended their friendship, they recall their early days in America. But Kobotsky, it is soon revealed, has not come for memories but for money; and this fact
fills Lieb with apprehension and Bessie with horror. In fury, as
she swirls about the room, she recalls to the anguished Lieb the
deceptiveness of their prosperity, the bills, the impending opera-
tion on his eyes. Kobotsky, rising like a ghost, prepares to leave;
but he stops long enough to pour out a tale of woe. The money
would have been used, he tells them, to purchase a stone for the
grave of his wife, dead more than five years.

As Kobotsky catalogues his misery, it is not only Lieb who
cries but Bessie as well. For a moment, the baker is reassured:
"She would now say yes, give the money, and they would all
sit down at the table and eat together." But the last word is
not Lieb's nor Kobotsky's. The finale belongs to Bessie, and it is
her tale which transforms the incipient sentimentality into a
dreadful glance at demonic frustrations:

> But Bessie, though weeping, shook her head, and before they
> could guess what, had blurted out the story of her afflictions:
> how the Bolsheviki came when she was a little girl and dragged
> her beloved father into the snowy fields without his shoes;
> the shots scattered the blackbirds in the trees and the snow
> oozed blood; how, when she was married a year, her husband,
> a sweet and gentle man, an educated accountant—rare in those
> days and that place—died of typhus in Warsaw; and how she,
> abandoned in her grief, years later found sanctuary in the home
> of an older brother in Germany, who sacrificed his own chances
> to send her, before the war, to America, and himself ended,
> with wife and daughter, in one of Hitler's incinerators. (190)

Against Bessie's past and her wretched dream of the future,
Kobotsky's woe expends itself. Woe and woe, fused together
in opposition, deny them the expression of anything but compassion. As the loaves in Lieb's ovens turn into "charred corpses,"
Kobotsky and the baker embraced ". . . and pressed mouths
together and parted forever" (191).

"The Bill" and "The Loan" thus share alike the terrible con-
sequences of morality and poverty in collision; and both gain
their power from the nature of the theme itself: the horror
attendant on the frustration of man's need to give. Another fable

in the collection also sounds the same message, but it does so with such unmitigated directness that, like "The Mourners," it is more dismal than affecting. Entitled "Take Pity," the story is narrated in a sustained and brilliant Yiddish idiom, and tells how Rosen sought to give all to the widow Eva and her children; and, because of her repeated rejections, he finally assigns his possessions to her and commits suicide. But now in limbo, and narrating the story to Davidov, the census taker, Rosen and the widow suffer a weird turnabout. Having nothing left to give, Rosen inveighs against Eva who pleads for him with upraised arms: "Whore, bastard, bitch," he shouts at her. "Go 'way from here" (95).

That "Take Pity" falls short of the other two stories stems in part from the discrepancy between the abrupt conclusion and the supporting structure. Most of all, however, it fails because the author's own voice is missing. In the better fables, it is primarily his voice which lends the ambience of religious sensibility—enough at any rate to convince us that, as in "The Loan" and in "The Bill," the world may pervert the overt act but not the resources of communion. But in "Take Pity" Malamud employs, for the first time in his career, extended first person narration. With his own voice gone, the story slips quickly into an almost Gothic evocation.

IV The New York Tales Without Jews

What is most revealing about Malamud's difficulties in manipulating the fable form, however, stems from his attempts to apply it to an investigation of similar themes without Jewish characters, as in "The Prison" and in "A Summer's Reading." The first, the better of the two, is again concerned with the accidents which despoil communion. Trapped in a candy store (the prison of the piece) by his criminal past and by an arranged marriage, Tommy Castelli seems in many ways a prototype of Frankie Alpine—a young man yearning for release from the blight of possibilities. Unable himself to escape, Tommy in part discovers the means of salvation through a surrogate, a ten-year-old girl who steals candy from the shop, and who Tommy dreams of rescuing from the mistakes which had forced him into his time-rotting corner of the world. Though he prepares for the moment of confrontation with calculation, his wife discovers the girl's thievery: When Tommy interferes in the child's behalf, he finds himself refuted not only by his wife but by the girl herself.

In the same fashion as Tommy, George Stoyonovich, the young man of "A Summer's Reading," seeks unavailingly to escape the prison of self and a jobless East Side existence by telling his friends that he is spending the summer reading a hundred books. For the lie, George reaps the respect of his neighbors and a bemusing sense of personal worth. But the lie quickly turns rank when George realizes that Mr. Cattanzara, an early father image, suspects his dishonesty. George flees the recognition, but Mr. Cattanzara proves to be a giver of trust, one of those elderly saints whose goodness forces its way into the heart of its "victims." In the final paragraph George appears closeted in the public library, ticking off a hundred titles and settling down to a season of protracted reading.

While deft and compelling, both these stories are curiously unlike "The Loan" or "The Bill"; and the difference, of course, is the absence of a central Jewish character. Far from being a small difference, however, it accounts precisely for what the stories lack: the sense of the pertinacity of spirit, an indefinable aura of "goodness" which, through the agency of the Bobers and the Felds, transforms the most extreme of failures into a sad redemption. "The Prison" and "A Summer's Reading" are in fact naturalistic tales which reveal more of Malamud's virtuosity than his fundamental skills.

The same losses and gains are also apparent in the five remaining stories in *The Magic Barrel*—all of which either depart from the folk tale or seek to extend it into more elaborate and significant forms. Among them are Malamud's best and his worst stories, but even the worst possess power. The first, "The Girl of My Dreams," swings irresolutely between realism and symbolism; but it resolves itself ultimately into a farcical, ebullient account of the breakthrough into communalism of a shattered young Jewish novelist, Mitka by name, whose literary failure, curiously enough, has to do with an inability to record experience directly. Locked in his tiny room, Mitka tortures himself with the sense of failure and agonizes over his land-lady, Mrs. Lutz, who unavailingly bears love and chicken soup to his door. To all her entreaties, however, Mitka presents closed ears with a tenacity humorously reminiscent of Raskolnikov's masochistic misanthropy. But Mitka, for all his self-incarceration, is one of Malamud's fractured young men who find their need for love and communion welling up in a strangling ooze; and, while resisting it, they are ripe for success. Success comes, moreover, through the appearance of a mysterious female writer whose newspaper stories had deeply affected Mitka and with whom, half in love, he had arranged a meeting. But "the girl of my dreams" turns out to be no girl at all; instead, she is a "lone middle-aged female . . . Hefty . . . Eyeglassed, and marvelously plain" (36).

Mitka, however, is a man of character; and Olga, the "girl" of the story is also a cosmic mother. Steeling himself to her ordinary face, Mitka indulges in a lengthy colloquium, is fed, admired, and advised; and, under the influence of her faith, he opens like a spring flower. Returning home from the en-counter with this new version of Iris Lemon, a woman who had suffered her way into humanity, Mitka vows to go on with his writing; and, more importantly, he decides to fling wide his door to Mrs. Lutz with whom he imagines a new relationship: "They would jounce together up the stairs, then (strictly a one-marriage man) he would swing her across the threshold, holding her where the fat overflowed her corset as they waltzed around his writing chamber" (41).

Despite the humor, and the fact that "The Girl of My Dreams" is the first and only story in the collection to deal with sexual communion (one of Malamud's favorite novel subjects), the story remains, at best, only interesting. It lacks not only the concentrated effect of "The Loan" or "The Bill," but also the tangible persuasiveness that Malamud seems always to derive from his ancient Jews. The primary difference is of course Mitka himself, who, like S. Levin, is a young ostensible intellectual and so resists the kind of reduction to bedrock properties upon which Malamud's stories depend. To render Mitka viable to his theme, the author must rely too exclusively on satire and farcical symbolism—as, in fact, he does with almost all of his stories which deal with second-generation American Jews.

V *The Italian Stories*

This same problem, moreover, comes to the fore in two of the three stories in the collection which deal with young Americans in Italy, a setting which Malamud seems to delight in almost as much as in New York's East Side—and for similar reasons. At once real and fabled, Italy (and particularly Rome) surrounds the *angst*-ridden Malamud protagonist with the smell and detritus of ancient lore at the same time that it benumbs moral hunger with fanciful romance. In some ways, in fact, Italy serves Malamud in much the same way it served Henry James in his depiction of the naïve American in an international world: a fairyland supported by the thinnest of ice that, upon breaking, precipitates a plunge into depths of feeling hitherto overlooked, denied, or transmuted.

The first of these stories, "Behold the Key," is the most enigmatical. The protagonist, Carl Schneider, a student and a lover of things Italian, comes to Rome with his wife and children and spends his time, not with books, but in apartment hunting. Guided by an inexplicable Virgil, one of those shabby ministers of grace who frequently appear in Malamud's stories, Schneider encounters all manner of deceptions and intrigues, criminal landlords and outright knaveries until, at the end of his patience, a "perfect" apartment is found which can be his if he will tender a bribe. Carl refuses and not only loses the apartment but bears on his forehead the mark of the key thrown by the outraged former tenant, the individual who had insisted on the bribe.

If deceptive, there is at the heart of the story a grim, telling theme. What is being tested is not only Carl Schneider's patience but his humanity: his ability to understand the behavior of a people who, because of war and poverty, bear little resemblance to the literary curiosities that had nourished his dream of an ideal Italy. Because he fails to comprehend, he bears the mark of his failure—a failure of brotherhood—upon his brow.

The second of the Italian stories, which also deals with the failure of a young American in Europe, is perhaps closer to the center of the author's real interests in that it imports into the ancient setting a New York Jew: a thirty-year-old former book clerk who, "tired of the past—tired of the limitations imposed upon him," has come to Europe in search of adventure, romance, and, though he hardly dare name it, love (105). Entitled "The Lady of the Lake," the story is, like all the Italian pieces, longer, less concentrated, and more indebted to symbolist techniques than are the New York tales. Indeed, these stories which deal exclusively with young men in Europe clearly evoke in the author a technique closer to that of *The Natural* than to *The Assistant*.

However, the themes are the writer's in any setting. In "The Lady of the Lake" Henry Levin, who calls himself Henry R. Freeman, is precisely the kind of out-of-touch, past-denying, and self-denying specimen of incompletion that Malamud can stick wriggling to the wall with telling effect. Rushing through Europe, his heart bubbling with need, Levin finally finds romance and love (in a perfumed garden on the Isolo del Dongo) in the person of a hungry-eyed goddess, transparent with mystery, whom he takes to be Isabella del Dongo, last of a mighty lineage. To her unexpected question: "Are you, perhaps, Jewish?," Levin, cocking ear and eye to the future, replies that he is not (113). With romance flaming and wallowing through her further questions as to his Jewishness and his further denials, Levin pursues Isabella in a cloud of frustration and guilt. Needless to say, the guilt is ironic to the core, for what grieves Levin about his lie is his own Jewishness; and it is Jewishness finally which ends his happiness. In a penultimate meeting, Isabella tells Levin that she is not a del Dongo but a della Setta, child of poor people. Romance crucified, Levin retreats, his dreams shredded like confetti.

But with romance gone, love bounds to the fore, and Levin rushes back to the island to find Isabella waiting for him in a white dress. When he tells her he has come to offer marriage, she asks again if he is Jewish. Levin, his life trembling, flounders and denies it. The denial is catastrophe. Isabella suddenly unbuttons her bodice to reveal the marks of Buchenwald; and, as Levin stares, she tells him: "I can't marry you. We are Jews. My past is meaningful to me. I treasure what I suffered for." Though Levin-Freeman cries "I—I am," it is too late, for Isabella disappears into the mists which have risen from the lake. Levin, for his denial of self, embraces "only moonlit stone" (132-33).

Intensely funny and marked by a brilliantly controlled meta-

phorical style, "The Lady of the Lake" hovers of course directly
and illuminatingly over Malamud's chief preoccupations. But
neither the comedy nor the richness of theme obviates the fact
that it is, like "Behold the Key," far from his best work. Slick
in its manipulation of symbol and sparse in its "felt" experience,
the story is another case of the resultant weakness when Malamud
attempts to extend his themes into non-Jewish areas or into a
contemplation of the young and divided or intellectual Jew. In
the former case, the stories persist in dissolving into bitter
realism. In the latter, Malamud inevitably loses the tone and
perspective that clings to his contemplation of elderly Jews who
seek to expiate their "other." Toward Mitka and toward Levin,
as well as toward the Levin of *A New Life*, the author must
find, in lieu of the aged Jews of the better stories, some new
vehicle to supply conviction. And he finds it not in the resources
of character but in satire, irony, and a metaphorical style that
more often than not is strained and obvious.

VI *"The Last Mohican" and "The Magic Barrel"*

But what is lacking in "The Lady of the Lake" is assuredly
not absent from the concluding Italian story, "The Last Mohican,"
nor from the final story in the collection, "The Magic Barrel,"
which reverts to the New York setting but which also concen-
trates on a youthful Jewish protagonist. For in both these stories
Malamud has found a new character to further the redemptive
cycle: an aged Jew in place of an Iris Lemon, one who fastens
to the tormented heroes like a spiritual cannibal and does not
release his hold until the younger man submits to the terrors of
rebirth.

The first of the two stories details the old-world adventures of
Arthur Fidelman, a "self-confessed failure as a painter" (156)
who arrives in Italy clutching the pigskin brief case which contains the first chapter of a projected study of Giotto and wearing
the tweed suit and oxblood shoes which are the uniform of his
new identity as an art critic. As Fidelman stands on a street
corner staring at his reflection with an exalted sense of the future,
the image becomes compounded by the appearance of Shimon
Susskind—a knickered skeleton in "small porous, pointed shoes"
who at that moment becomes the catalyst which transforms the

young Jew's quest for a future identity into an unconscious but purgatorial descent into self (156).

Susskind is patently Malamud's most improbable minister of salvation. On the one hand a jack-of-all-trades and a master of most, he is also a refugee from all countries and a victim in each. Furthermore, he is an opportunist of fabulous proportions who tests Fidelman's humanity as severely as the Romans tested Carl Schneider. Intent from the initial meeting upon securing Fidelman's second but still serviceable suit, Susskind spends the first half of the story with hand outstretched, materializing magically ("How do I live? . . . I eat air." [164]) and regularly before Fidelman's pained eyes. When the critic gives, in lieu of his suit, money and meals, Susskind can only ask: "Not more?"

To Fidelman, the pursuit is torture. A man of awesome difficulties, the former painter unites in one person something of Mitka's problems—for his inability to paint is only the mark of the self's imprisonment—and of S. Levin's tormented search for a new life. Perpetually on guard against himself and his old habits, Fidelman nonetheless suffers as scraps of denied personality spill over either in short-lived ecstasy at the sights of Rome or in a thick pall of gloom. Matching his moods is always the magical Susskind, whose appearances inevitably catch Fidelman whenever his "new" self is functioning at its best. The pursuit comes to a climax when, in a restaurant, Fidelman poses a question which Susskind disposes of in short order. "Am I responsible for you then, Susskind?" asks Fidelman. Susskind replies: "Then you are responsible. Because you are a man. Because you are a Jew, aren't you?"

For Fidelman, who insists on eating spaghetti like the Italians, the answer is not easy. His reply in fact looks tentative: "I am a single individual and can't take on everybody's personal burden. I have the weight of my own to contend with" (165-66). The story exists, however, to demonstrate that "my own" is no respecter of limitations. In the same fashion as Frankie Alpine, Fidelman must discover that the way to the self is paradoxically through another; and the answer is heralded by a sudden alteration of the pursuit. After the scene of questioning, Susskind steals Fidelman's pigskin brief case and the precious first chapter; and it is now the young critic's turn to pursue.

The chase lasts for several days in which Fidelman alternately groans over his inability to study or rewrite his first chapter or combs the streets of the city for a sight of the knickered Susskind. Ironically, however, the "beginning" he searches for has already been usurped by a new one; and it is sealed in the course of the chase which even Fidelman suspects is not for the "chapter per se" (177). This ironic indeterminacy of goal underscores Fidelman's prolonged quest and transforms it into a wildly comic yet moving contretemps. Abandoning his tweed suit and oxblood shoes in favor of a beret and black pointed shoes (the very clothes Susskind wears), Fidelman disappears into the Roman ghettos where, following some intuitive Baedeker, he plunges out of romance and into the horrors of Jewish history, past and present, to end finally in a forelorn cemetery whose headstones testify to Nazi brutality. In the process, Fidelman, like a foetus, feeds and grows older and starts upward toward the light.

The pursuit is capped when Fidelman, who is now capable of sketching "little angels flying" (177), discovers Susskind's room. Like Morris Bober's store, it explains all—or nearly all. Rather than a room, it is a cave, "a pitch black freezing cave" (180), that seems less like a home than the Ardeatine caves. Back in his own comfortable rooms, it takes Fidelman hours to thaw out: "But from the visit he never fully recovered" (181). That night, Fidelman, in a flood of compassion, opens his heart in dreams, and over the dream hovers Susskind's early statement, "Who doesn't know Giotto?" (159). Only, it would seem, till now, Fidelman; for in the dream he finds himself, after having been led to the spot by "Virgilio Susskind," lying beneath one of the master's frescoes: "Giotto. San Francesco dona le vesti al cavaliere povero."

Fidelman awakes, stuffs his second suit into a bag, and carries it to Susskind. "Wear it in good health," he intones to the "cavaliere povero." As he turns lightheartedly to leave, Susskind comes after with his own offering—the pigskin brief case. Discovering that it is empty, Fidelman plays momentary host to the old demonic spirit: "You bastard, you burned my chapter!" Already in flight, Susskind, "light as the wind in his marvelous knickers," shouts back the final, and who can doubt it, true verdict upon Fidelman's earlier identity: "Have mercy, I did you a favor. . . . The words were there but the spirit was missing." For a moment Fidelman continues the chase, but the spirit he had lacked is no longer missing. With a "triumphant insight," he calls, "Susskind, come back. The suit is yours. All is forgiven." But the refugee, when last seen, was still running. (181-82).

By and large, "The Last Mohican" has the neat advantage, like Fidelman himself, of unifying the elements in "Behold the Key" and "The Lady of the Lake," and yet reasserting them in a more successful manner. In a sense, the work cuts across both the two earlier Italian stories, for Fidelman's task is to find, as Carl Schneider could not, the sources of compassion and humanity; and like Henry Levin-Freeman, Fidelman finds them in a descent into his true self. Moreover, that Malamud has himself discovered the literary means for unifying these elements, and in the process makes of the Italian setting a more capable frame for his themes, is clearly the result of opening the form to the Jewish parable that he always handles with consummate skill. "The Last Mohican" indicates not only the full range of Malamud's concerns but, equally important, it illustrates the direction he must take to accommodate and enlarge them in more convincing literary structures.

Yet it must be said before leaving the first collection that even without "The Last Mohican," or for that matter even without "The Bill" or "The Loan"—the work would still contain sufficient evidence of the reach of Malamud's art. The title story, which is also the last story in the collection, would alone serve; for it is not only the finest piece in the collection, uniting all that is best in the other stories, but is perhaps one of the finest stories of recent years.

The impact of "The Magic Barrel" is, however, inexplicable —certainly as inexplicable, and for much the same reasons, as *The Assistant.* The story of the love and maturation of a young rabbinical student, it conspires like the author's second novel in a boundary world which pulsates now with the bright energy of a fairy tale, now with something of the somber tones of a depression tract. Both qualities are immediately apparent in the opening: "Not long ago there lived in uptown New York, in a small, almost meager room, though crowded with books, Leo Finkle, a rabbinical student in the Yeshivah University" (193).

The key to Leo Finkle's rebirth, however, lies not alone in the protagonist, a poor and lonely student hurrying after six years of study toward his June ordination. A Frankie Alpine in a black fedora, Leo unites myth and anti-myth in his own person. Passionately interested in Jewish law since childhood, Leo is nonetheless Godless. Bound in his deceit, he throbs through the torment that washes over Malamud's love-hungry and God-hungry young Jews. Like Fidelman on Giotto, Finkle knows the word but not the spirit; and he makes it clear in every gesture that in a secret part of his heart he knows it.

But Leo Finkle's heart is too secretive, and his salvation depends upon another who can test all there is of humanity in the student. The "other" does not arrive, however, until the last page; in her place there comes a marriage broker whom Leo has summoned when he learns that a wife will help him win a congregation. But from the moment Pinye Salzman materializes, the student is on the way. For, reeking of fish and business, the broker seems only another Susskind. Half criminal, half messenger of God, Salzman whips from his battered portfolio a select group of feminine portraits, for "is every girl good for a new rabbi?"

As Pinye exalts his merchandise, however, Leo persists in positing reservations; and they are not alone a matter of distrusting Salzman's grossness (indeed, he seems *too* gross to be believed). When Pinye plays his trump card: "Ruth K., Nineteen years, Honor student. Father offers thirteen thousand cash to the right bridegroom," Leo, sick of the whole business, gives himself away: "But don't you think this young girl believes in love?" (197-98).

Dismissing Pinye, Leo slides into misery; but the misery is only the signal of breaking ice. Trying to analyze his reactions, he wonders if perhaps "he did not, in essence, care for the matchmaking institution?" (199). From this thought, slightly heretical, he flees throughout the day; and it is only at nightfall, when he draws out his books, that he finds any peace. But Pinye, like a haggard ghost—and he grows more desperate-looking with each meeting—is soon at the door, his presence thrusting Leo out of his books and threadbare composure. Bearing the vitae of Lily Hirschorn, high-school teacher and linguist, young (twenty-nine instead of the thirty-two of the night before), Pinye dispels

Leo's lack of interest with a mournful imprecation: "Yiddishe kinder, what can I say to somebody that he is not interested in high school teachers?" (201).

Despite the retiring young scholar's hesitancy, a meeting is arranged; and one Saturday afternoon he strides along Riverside Drive with Lily Hirschorn, oldish but pretty, hanging to his arm. From the beginning, however, Leo senses the presence of Pinye, somewhere in the background, perhaps "flashing the lady signals with a pocket mirror; or perhaps a cloven-hoofed Pan, piping nuptial ditties."

But if Pinye is directing the proceedings, he is after more than a quick profit; for about the walk there is strong suggestion of ritual indoctrination, a testing by question and answer that suddenly exposes Leo. Lily, having been primed by Salzman into the belief that Leo Finkle is the true anointed of God (or is Lily another Iris?) addresses herself as if to a holy image: "How was it that you came to your calling?" When Leo, after some trepidation, replies, "I was always interested in the Law," Lily's questions soar: "When did you become enamored of God?" In mingled rage at Pinye and himself, Leo finds himself speaking with shattering honesty: "I am not a talented religious person. I think that I came to God not because I loved Him, but because I did not" (202-4).

After the smoke-screen of hatred for Pinye dissipates, there is a long week of "unaccountable despair" in which Leo's beard grows ragged and his books meaningless. Feeding on his confession to Lily, which had revealed "to himself more than her—the true nature of his relationship to God," Leo bounds to further revelations. He realized that, "apart from his parents, he had never loved anyone." Then, with a quick jolt, the two ragged ends of his lovelessness fuse: "Or perhaps it went the other way, that he did not love God so well as he might, because he had not loved man" (205).

Made desperate by the unexpected image of himself, Leo contemplates leaving Yeshivah. "He had lived without knowledge of himself, and never in the Five Books and all the Commentaries—mea culpa—had the truth been revealed to him." The knowledge sends Leo scurrying into near hysteria, a state disagreeable and pleasurable at the same time, and then into a long swoon, a kind of moral way-station from which he "drew

the consolation that he was a Jew and that a Jew suffered."
The revelation, needless to say, represents a turning; and
when Salzman returns—at precisely this moment—he must listen
to a new Leo: "I want to be in love with the one I marry. . . . I
find it necessary to establish the level of my need and fulfill it."
Discharged, Salzman disappears "as if on the wings of the wind";
but he leaves behind a manila packet (205-7).

The pattern of pursuit which dominates the first half of "The
Magic Barrel" parallels also the early sections of "The Last
Mohican"; moreover, like Fidelman's in the Italian story, Leo
Finkle's redemption involves the reversal of the pattern, the
quest of the once despised. Coincident with the arrival of March
and the turning toward spring, Finkle remains closeted in his
room, gloomy over the frustrations of his hopes for a better life;
and so, finally, he is drawn to open the manila packet which
had all the while been gathering dust. Within he finds more
photographs, but all seem versions of Lily Hirschorn. But, as the
scholar puts them back, he discovers another snapshot, small
and cheap, which without preliminaries evokes a shout of love.
Staring back at him is a composite of every heroine Malamud
has yet written about, from Iris Lemon and Harriet Bird through
Pauline Gilley and Helen Bober. In shreds of images, some
mythic, some terrifyingly real, the face closes, like fate itself, over
Leo's heart:

> . . . spring flowers, yet age—a sense of having been used to the
> bone, wasted; this came from the eyes, which were hauntingly
> familiar, yet absolutely strange. He had a vivid impression that
> he had met her before, but try as he might he could not place
> her although he could almost recall her name, as if he had read
> it in her own handwriting. . . . *something* about her moved
> him . . . she leaped forth to his heart—had *lived,* or wanted to—
> more than just wanted, perhaps regretted how she had lived—
> had somehow deeply suffered. . . . Her he desired . . . he
> experienced fear of her and was aware that he had received an
> impression, somehow, of evil. (208-9)

Dashing into the streets, Leo rushes off in pursuit of Pinye
Salzman, only to discover from his wife (and "He could have
sworn he had seen her, too, before but knew it was an illusion"),
that the matchmaker was nowhere about, that he "lived in the

air." "Go home," she suggests, "he will find you." When the student returns to his flat, Salzman, standing at the door, asks, "You found somebody you like?" Without hestitation, Finkle extends the snapshot. But for his eager love the student must submit to the final horror. With a groan, Pinye tells him "this is not a bride for a rabbi . . . She is a wild one—wild, without shame." When Finkle presses Salzman for a clearer answer, the old man dissolves in tears: "This is my baby, my Stella, she should burn in hell" (210-12).

Under the covers of his bed, a makeshift chapel perilous, Leo, beating his breast, undergoes the climactic test. "Through days of torment he endlessly struggled not to love her; fearing success he escaped it. He then concluded to convert her to goodness, himself to God. The idea alternately nauseated and exalted him." Though brief, the ordeal finally draws Leo from bed with a long "pointed beard" and "eyes weighted with wisdom." A mixture now of lover and father, he meets Salzman again (and the marriage broker seems unaccountably young) and, despite Salzman's pleas to desist, a meeting is arranged.

The rendezvous, held on a spring night, is Malamud at his ambiguous best. With flowers in hand, Leo finds Stella standing in the age-old posture of the prostitute, under a lamp post smoking: "She waited uneasily and shyly. From afar he saw that her eyes—clearly her father's—were filled with desperate innocence. He pictured, in her, his own redemption. Violins and lit candles revolved in the sky. Leo ran foward with flowers outstretched."

This paragraph, however, is the penultimate one: as if the mixture of goddess and prostitute, the promise of hope through a future of willfully chosen agony, were not sufficiently confusing, Malamud allows the final paragraph to focus on Pinye, who, leaning upon a wall around the corner, "chanted prayers for the dead." It is impossible to tell for whom Pinye chants—for himself and his guilt (for even Leo had finally suspected "that Salzman had planned it all to happen this way"), for Finkle's past or Finkle's future, or for all these reasons. In some ways, the last alternative—that Salzman chants for everything—seems only proper; for if Leo has graduated into saint and rabbi, it is only by succumbing to the terrors which the role prescribes. What better reason to chant when to win means to lose?

But such confusions, as demonstrated in *The Assistant,* are the only possible vehicles for Malamud's faith. If the ironies undercutting the story preserve it from a kind of mythic schmaltz, the myth preserves the story from the irony. The same strange tension is surely in the characters—in the infected goddesses, like Stella, who can only be redeemed by the hero as victim, and in those unstable ministers of God, now devils and now angels, the Pinye Salzmans and the Shimon Susskinds. In that inexplicable and indeterminate character, they signal, as Alfred Kazin has said, "the unforeseen possibilities of the human—when everything seems dead set against it."[7] One finishes "The Magic Barrel" as one finishes *The Assistant*—not with the exaltation of witnessing miracles, but with the more durable satisfaction of witnessing possibilities.

Idiots First

Five years after the publication of *The Magic Barrel* Malamud published his second volume of stories, *Idiots First.* As was to be expected, both the fame of the first collection and the expectations of Malamud's large audience resulted in some curious critical reactions. For many, the later stories seemed only a continuation of the earlier ones (a fact which perhaps accounts for the large number of unfavorable reviews); but for others the relationship of the two volumes seemed singularly unclear.

While it is probably too soon to hope for an adequate assessment of Malamud's latest work, the second response seems more appropriate. Of the eleven stories in *Idiots First,* only two belong to the period in which the earliest stories in *The Magic Barrel* were written. One of the pieces first appeared in 1957, the same year as *The Assistant;* but the remaining eight belong to the 1960's. Because of this it is possible to use the single volume as a means of comparing Malamud's "older" manner with his new; and, by and large, the work demands such a comparison. For while it is evident that the author's themes in his latest work are a direct echo of the earlier stories, the means he employs to liberate them often strike new and vital ground.

Perhaps the most obvious symptom of this change lies in the absence of those remarkable fables like "The Loan" and "The Bill" which represent some of the most impressive achievements in *The Magic Barrel*. Only two stories in the new collection, "The Cost of Living" (first published in 1949) and "The Death of Me" (first published in 1950), employ the folk-tale form which Malamud had perfected in his first volume. "The Cost of Living" seems, in fact, to be a preliminary sketch for *The Assistant*—a tale which recounts how Sam Tomashevsky, an old and gentle grocer, was ruined by a neighboring supermarket and a guilt-wracked landlord. In the second, and the better story, the reader is also on familiar ground. One of those tragi-comic little tales (recalling, as many of Malamud's critics have indicated, Marc Chagall's affecting blend of bitter comedy and wistful nostalgia), "The Death of Me" is concerned with a saintly old clothier's efforts to reconcile his two warring assistants. Both stories, needless to say, are powerful; and even if not so powerful as the better tales in *The Magic Barrel*, they serve as clear reminders of the earlier collection.

VII   *The Transformation of the Early Fables*

But what is so instructive about the new volume is that, beyond these two pieces, the fable form either disappears entirely or survives by virtue of a rather remarkable transformation that appears in two more recent stories—the title piece and "The Jewbird," both of which were written within the last few years. In both cases, it is quite clear that Malamud's interest in the semi-folk tale persists only by virtue of his ability to undo or perhaps exaggerate the weird mixture of fictional modes which made the earlier stories so memorable.

"Idiots First," which begins the collection, is a case in point. Though structurally it *seems* like the early fables, the resemblance is more deceptive than real. Indeed, the story seems somehow less a case of Malamud the neo-folk realist than a case of Malamud the writer of moralities. And that, precisely, is what "Idiots First" is: a morality *à la Everyman* in which the sense of a real world (if only the sense of it) is utterly absorbed by a dream-landscape, a never-never-land New York City through which an elderly Jew named Mendel wanders in search of comfort and aid. Where the settings in the earlier stories threatened to disappear, in "Idiots First" the threat is realized

A summary of the plot clarifies the differences. Mendel is not only a dying man but one who has made a compact with death (personified by a bearded Jew, Ginzburg) and has been given part of an evening in which to gather the thirty-five dollars needed to send his idiot son to an uncle in California. The story, which follows the father from the moment he draws on "his cold embittered clothing"[8] to the moment he confronts Ginzburg at the train depot, is a striking mixture of gothicism and sudden touches of realism. After an encounter with a "red bearded" pawnbroker who stinks of fish and inhumanity, Mendel conveys his son Isaac to the home of the wealthy Fishbein, a philanthropist who gives money *only* to institutions, and who orates in a masterly mixture of dialect and phony phrases: "Show this party where is the door—unless he wishes to partake food before leaving the premises" (8).

Failing with Fishbein, Mendel hurries through a strange park in which leafless trees reverse their branches, runs screaming from a stranger (Ginzburg) who shouts "Gut yuntif," and ends up at a synagogue where a dying rabbi, resisting his young wife, allows Mendel to steal his fur-lined kaftan and then is stricken with a heart attack. From there Mendel flees to the pawnbroker and at last to the station where the California-bound train is about to leave. However, Mendel is past the appointed hour. Ginzburg stands before the gate, barring the way to the train, and resists the old man's pleas in a voice edged with doom and guilt: "I ain't in the anthropomorphic business. . . . The law is the law." But Mendel, wasted and past his time, is also the carrier of human possibilities. Like a gnarled Prometheus he seizes Ginzburg by the throat, shouting, "You bastard, don't you understand what it means human?" Ginzburg, about to destroy the old man, sees in Mendel's eyes his own iron wrath and relents long enough for Mendel to place Isaac on the train and return (13-15).

Though there are echoes in its form of such pieces as "The Loan" or "The First Seven Years," the story creates a totally different experience. If in the earlier stories the author seemed an East Side Anderson, in "Idiots First" he seems an East Side Bunyan. What is most curious, however, is that where "Idiots First" undoes the close unity of the fables by placing comparatively real characters in wildly imaginary gardens, the second of the transformed fables, "The Jewbird," reverses the process. The setting of "The Jewbird" is real enough—Harry Cohen's apartment near the lower East River; but the protagonist is a bedraggled crow-like Jewbird named Schwartz who one evening flies into the kitchen and to Harry Cohen's preliminary swat cries: "Gevalt, a pogrom!" (102). Beyond the initial shock, however, the story unfolds in a manner strikingly realistic; and it is soon clear that if Schwartz is a bird, he is also an exemplary image of the Malamudian victim. Half Bober and half Susskind, Schwartz is constantly pursued by anti-Semites and by fate. Moreover, and most importantly, Schwartz is also the compound image of opportunist and saint who tests to the extreme the humanity and the compassion of others.

In particular it is Harry Cohen, head of his family (a wife Edie, and a not-so-bright son, Maurie) who is tested. Stubbornly resisting Schwartz's presence, the effluvia of herring, the woebegone look of misery—as well as the bird's usurpation of his role as father—Cohen loathes Schwartz from his first appearance. As Cohen's guilt feeds an ever-growing hatred, his schemes to torture Schwartz become more diabolical. The climax occurs one winter evening when Cohen throws the bird from the window and in the process flings redemption, wisdom, and fatherhood with it. Later, in the spring, the weeping Maurie recovers the battered body, and when he begs his mother to name the murderers he receives the eloquent reply: "Anti-Semeets" (113).

Like "Idiots First," "The Jewbird" retains the frame of Malamud's earlier short stories but largely alters the sense of reality. Because of this difference, it is difficult to measure the power of either tale. Of the effectiveness of the first, its deft application of allegory to Jewish themes, as well as its refined sense of terror, there can be little question. Nor can there be any question of the comic gifts in "The Jewbird." The style is delightful, and the reader succumbs willingly to its sustained realism-within-madness. But however that may be, neither story is so successful as the better pieces in *The Magic Barrel;* and the reasons seem peculiarly a matter of the self-conscious exaggeration of technique which, ultimately, does not support the conclusions. In "The Jewbird," the naturalistic end is simply too flat: the inevitable fall is too traditional to overcome the weight of the fantasy. The conclusion of "Idiots First" is similarly marred.

One suspects finally that the allegorical presentation has teased Malamud into a victory he could hardly have employed in his earlier stories—or perhaps only in a fantasy such as "Angel Levine." Though more powerful than "The Jewbird," "Idiots First" ends at the moment Mendel leaps at Ginzburg's throat and not, as Malamud has it, when Ginzburg relents. The conclusion is not Malamud at his rigorous best—at those moments when he must rescue affirmation out of the inevitabilities of natural law. In succumbing to the temptations of allegory, Malamud has not only invested his vision of human misery with a new horror but, paradoxically, with a new optimism.

However, it is unnecessary to press the point because Malamud himself seems to have grown disenchanted with the form. Of the remaining seven stories, four are Italian pieces, one is a tale of a college professor which is strongly reminiscent of *A New Life*, and, most importantly, two are very recent stories which resist close comparison with any of Malamud's earlier works.

VIII *The Later Italian Stories*

The four Italian stories may also be divided into separate categories. Two of them, among the longest stories in the collection, concern the further adventures of Arthur Fidelman, and they are the wildest and most bizarre tales Malamud has yet written. It is in fact impossible to deal with them seriously. Whatever the author's original plans for Fidelman may have been, he has turned him into his own special clown, a sour-faced perpetually troubled grotesque who, if the course of his progress through these two stories can be projected into further adventures, is bound upon a furiously revolving wheel of periodic ecstasies, depressions, and sudden delirious victories.

Both stories are too long and too complicated to be discussed at length. The first of them, "Still Life," is a sad-absurd sexual travesty which finds Fidelman, a painter living in a Roman garret, lustfully in love with his *pittrice*, another of those sweet-sour neurotic images of grieving incompletion. Her name, in point of fact, is Annamaria Oliovino. Mashed to incoherent deviltry by her own faith and her past sins, Anna takes from Fidelman everything but his person and keeps him bounding from hope to despair. Their relationship comes to a head when

Fidelman, riding the crest of a revelation, decides to portray himself as a priest; in the guise of the father, he elicits from Annamaria both her love and the secrets of her past. Far from being a virgin, as Fidelman had once in his romantic love portrayed her, she reveals that she had borne a child out of wedlock and in terror had thrown it into the Tiber River. For a moment all balances upon Fidelman's silence; but, finally, secure in his cassock and his love, he speaks the proper words: "I forgive you, my child." In an abrupt concluding paragraph, one bewildering in its mixture of passion and compassion, Malamud unites spirit and flesh: "Annamaria undressed in a swoop. Her body was extraordinarily lovely, the flesh glowing. In her bed they tightly embraced. She clasped his buttocks, he cupped hers. Pumping slowly he nailed her to her cross" (56).

Needless to say, it is difficult to distinguish in this mish-mash of lust and ritual copulation the strains of opportunism from real victory. And the same problem, if indeed it *is* a problem, besets the second and better of the Fidelman stories, "Naked Nude," which was also written in the early 1960's. In this story Fidelman is a prisoner in a third-rate hotel and brothel in Milan, guarded by the proprietor and his homosexual second. Offered his freedom if he will execute a copy of Titian's "Venus of Urbino" which his captors can substitute for the original, the freedom-yearning moralist agrees. The painting, however, will not materialize. For like Mitka in his writing, Fidelman can only render a realistic portrait of a woman if love guides his brush. Indeed, in both the Fidelman stories abstract painting seems to be the result of either the absence of human affection or of the unintegrated personality.

In anxiety, therefore, Fidelman doodles unavailingly on the canvas until, rising from a dream, he has "A stupendous thought . . . Suppose he personally were to steal the picture?" Fidelman's decision, which follows the fact that he has fallen in love with the Venus of the original, is equivalent to integration. In a furious bout with the canvas he turns out a perfect copy. Later, he accompanies one of his captors to the Isola Bella, apparently substitutes his own portrait for the original, and exits with his henchman to the rowboat that is to carry them to safety. At the last moment, however, Fidelman knocks his guard on the head; boards the boat, and is last seen starting a sixty-kilometer row to Locarno and freedom. But with which portrait? There are only clues and no answers; and if the reader suspects that Fidelman has stolen his own painting, it can never finally be more than a suspicion. Whatever the real answer may be, it must either wait the appearance of future tales of Fidelman or rest in its own ambiguity.

But if such ambiguity is central to Malamud's portrait of victory, the case is somewhat different in the Fidelman stories. Even though the author preserves in both the ritual of *naif* into father, and also manages to make a dozen points at once—to criticize abstract art, to discourse on the problems of flesh and spirit, to make some telling comments on the nature of sin and expiation—it is still difficult to believe the stories are anything but comic interludes. To take them seriously is perhaps to take them as flat failures. They look like nothing so much as the writer's own special area of literary recreation, a kind of wanton, ebullient field in which he can simply "let go" with that lethal style which appears only in *The Natural* and in sections of *A New Life*. If compelling in their wild comedy, the Fidelman stories bear out what was said of *A New Life*: when Malamud deals exclusively with young and fractured Jews, a bizarre and fantastic symbolism seems automatically to arise. That the rhetoric is motivated by moral concerns, that it is a celebration of the spirit's power to overcome the weight of countering reality in an elated leap, has already been shown; but in the case of Fidelman without Susskind, the power to soar suddenly in a comic-absurd-redemptive flight beyond one's limitations is less a matter of the mystery of character than the mystery of style. One may admire the author's technique, but can never be in awe of it. In his short stories Malamud has so largely avoided this problem that the Fidelman pieces come as a distinct shock. Aside from sections of "The Girl of My Dreams" or "The Lady of the Lake," *The Magic Barrel* was almost free of it; as for the remainder of the Italian stories in *Idiots First*, there is not a trace of this Malamud. Indeed, these stories seem in their muted ironies to belong to another genre entirely—and not even the closest reading of them can evoke the shadow of "Naked Nude" or "Still Life."

This difference is especially true of "Life is Better than Death," which, while centered in Rome, is as somber and low-pitched in

its way as "A Summer's Reading" or "The Prison." In this story
of a simple Italian woman who has retreated from life after the
death of her husband, Malamud hides horror in deliberate understatement. Etta, having prayed for Armando's death because of
his adultery, seeks atonement by endless prayers and regular
visits to her spouse's grave. During her visits to the cemetery
she meets the agent of her re-entry into the world, Cesare
Montaldo, who himself mourns a dead and adulterous mate and
who woos Etta with a strange mixture of ardor and truth:
". . . the truth is my wife was a pig. Your husband was a pig.
We mourn because we hate them. Let's have the dignity to
face the facts" (98). In an abruptly foreshortened conclusion,
Etta, convinced by Cesare, awakes to her own needs and sleeps
with her fellow mourner. At this point, however, the cycle of
redemption is blighted. In time Etta becomes pregnant; and
though Cesare vows he will acknowledge the child, he moves
away and leaves no address. The story's conclusion, a single short
paragraph, represents a deeper plunge into imprisonment than
before; while Etta once more lives only in a relationship with
a dead husband, the sense of her own adultery prevents her
from appearing at his grave.

"Life is Better than Death" is frankly depressing; its sense of
cruel loss is unusual for Malamud even at his most pessimistic.
Although the tale serves in this regard as a neat counter to the
Fidelman stories, it can hardly be called successful. In effect, it
recasts the problems of "Still Life" in reverse. Of all Malamud's
stories—not even excepting the realistic tales in *The Magic
Barrel*—"Life is Better than Death" is the most deficient in a
sense of character. Instead of sensibility turning the plot, the
plot take precedence over the actors; and there is about the
entire story, and not just the shock ending, a sense of machine-
like contrivance.

But perhaps the real reason for the failure of "Life is Better
than Death" is the absence of "the international theme," which
seems finally the author's fundamental technique for keeping
alive, in a new context, the drama of hidden sensibilities at war
which lies at the heart of all his best work. This fact is made
strikingly clear by a comparison of "Life is Better than Death"
with the last of the Italian stories, "The Maid's Shoes," which,

while as spare as the former piece, is really the strongest of the stories in the collection.

Written in 1957, "The Maid's Shoes" belongs to the same period as most of the better stories in *The Magic Barrel;* and, as in them, the real drama of the tale is a test in which compassion seeks, and in this case fails, to break through an imprisoning self. Set in Rome, the story recounts the brief contact of an aging but still pretty Italian maid and her American employer, a visiting scholar and authority on law. The test is designed for this sixty-year-old *isolato* who is neither good nor bad, but nervous with unexpressed need. Like his name, Orlando Krantz, the professor is frozen between opposing claims. Having hired Rosa to put his world in order until his wife and daughter return from a visit to the United States, Krantz finds himself attracted to the maid, in particular to her weight of sorrow, at the same time that he retreats in distrust: "These people had endless troubles, and if you let yourself get involved in them you got endlessly involved" (160).

Though the muted style never does more than suggest, the drama is pure Malamud. In the daily ritual of work, Krantz and Rosa whirl together in a relationship that is extremely confusing: a kind of mock marriage in which she cleans and cares and he rises periodically and nervously from his desk to observe her out of distrust and some inexplicable desire that he cannot, in fear, name. As in *The Assistant,* the narrative alternates from Krantz to Rosa and back again, but only rarely does it interpenetrate.

Of the two, Rosa's problems are "realest." In despair over the behavior of her son, as well as her poverty, she is, like the Italians in "Behold the Key," a patent symbol of human need sent to exorcise the inhumanities and frustrations of the American. But Krantz, though drawn by her sadness, continuously retreats from her desire to tell him of her woe; and he pleads internally: "I am sympathetic to your condition but I don't want to hear about it" (160). If an authority on law, Krantz clearly refuses to consider himself in the "anthropomorphic business"; and the division persists until Rosa, who "would not have it so" (160), one day breaks through his reserve long enough to tell him she is being wooed by a married man with a family who has promised to give her a new pair of shoes in place of the wretched pair she has worn for six years. She wants them, she tells the professor, but fears her acceptance will lead her to the man's bed.

The confession prompts the old scholar to act. Despite his fears (*re* Finkle and Salzman) that she has planned the whole thing, he presents her with a new pair of serviceable but unflattering brogues (their simplicity, like Fidelman's oxblood shoes, is the mark of the pragmatic, not the enthusiastic, spirit). A few hours later, however, Krantz discovers that Rosa has also accepted a pair—"dress black needlepoint pumps" (164)—from the married man; and in anger at her opportunism, though clearly also for reasons of unacknowledged jealousy, he fires her. Because of this act, Krantz immediately plunges into a week of nervousness. Though he cannot yet name his needs— nor ever shall—he takes Rosa back when she returns in tears to plead for the job and promises to end the relationship with Armando, the rival giver of gifts. In the ensuing days the relationship enters an even more confused period in which Rosa's stifled pains become more obvious and the professor, his reserve unconsciously relenting, offers additional money and food from his own larder.

At this point the story reaches a sudden climax. One "dismal" day Rosa confesses to Krantz that she is pregnant by Armando; and though in Krantz' eyes "her white underwear shone through her black dress," his voice is automatic: "You must leave at once" (166). To her pleas that she cannot return to her son, the scholar agrees to advance her two thousand lire so she can be examined by a doctor. The next day, however, Rosa reports that she has spent the money for a birthday gift for her worthless son.

In desperation Krantz himself takes Rosa to a neighboring doctor, learns that she is not pregnant, and sends her packing once and for all: "I simply cannot be constantly caught up in this sort of thing. It upsets me and I can't work" (169-70). With the professor looking on in wretched silence, Armando appears and ushers Rosa out of Krantz' apartment and his life. Later, Krantz enters the maid's room and discovers the drab shoes he had given her have been left behind.

Though flat and somber throughout, "The Maid's Shoes" hides its misery and loss just beneath the surface. It is a totally successful story, and one in which each gesture and scene and intonation of voice carries its full weight of irony and pain. Distinctively Malamud—a record of the unacknowledged self brought to the surface and there defeated by the weight of past habits and insecurities—it is something more as well; for, technically, the story is like few of the author's other works. The real source of its dramatic power, in fact, lies in the illusive nature of the narrator himself. In only a few of Malamud's stories is the sense of authorial distance so marked; and in even fewer of his stories is his control of the material, his objectivity, so insistent. The method is purely scenic. Despite this presentation, however, "The Maid's Shoes" manages to make its points through the characters, as do the better stories in *The Magic Barrel*. All in all, "The Maid's Shoes" is his most successful attempt to extend the distinctive concerns of the Jewish stories into non-Jewish characters in a non-Jewish world.

It is probably unnecessary to add that the absence of both the author's own mediation and the Jewish characters of the fables has important effects on the outcome of the stories. If the absence of saintly Jews ensures the author's "distance," it also conditions the conclusions. The Jewish fables may at times end in defeat, in the irrevocable locking of the door, but at the same time the author's wry and bittersweet tone succeeds in investing them with the sense of rare victory. But the non-Jewish stories, deprived of the narrator's presence and the resources of Jewish agony, most often end in total defeat. Perhaps the best example of this, aside from "The Maid's Shoes" and "Life is Better Than Death," is the late story (1963) "A Choice of Profession," which recounts the same history as that in *A New Life* but does so with a crucial alteration. Instead of the bumbling S. Levin, the hero of "A Choice of Profession" is named Cronin; and, for all *his* suffering, his retreat from the Northern California College community where he had sought a new life is not a victory but a dismal failure.

Like S. Levin, Cronin is a man hungering for love and victimized by a twisted past, who has traveled west in order to refashion himself through teaching English, a profession he had always considered "religious . . . it had something to do with giving oneself to others" (70). But Cronin is quickly disappointed, both by his classes and by himself. Through a dry season he nurses his discontent until, in spring, a new student appears and tosses him into the mythic mill. Her name is Mary Lou Miller; and despite the brevity of the story, she is a clear instance of the damaged goddesses who offer Malamud's heroes agonized fulfillment. Having herself survived a monstrous past, Mary Lou does not hesitate to confess it to Cronin on their first date. She tells him that she had once been a prostitute but has remade herself.

Because of her confession, however, Cronin rejects her advances at the same time that he is dazzled by her selflessness. But Cronin's needs cannot be downed; indeed, though he cannot admit it to himself, he has fallen in love with Mary Lou. The second meeting, replete with a day at a lake, ends with a further confession: as they are about to enter her apartment, Mary Lou tells him that she had once had an incestuous affair with her brother. Cronin recoils again—this time with a shout that echoes back to "The Bill": "Don't trust me"—and drops into a series of anguished days in which he nurses his love for Mary Lou and yet continues to reject it. When Cronin sees her with a fellow professor, his heart is flooded with jealousy. In return for telling the man of Mary Lou's past, he is thanked profusely: "It wouldn't pay to get involved" (85).

One final meeting remains. Suspecting Cronin's interference, Mary Lou confronts the unhappy teacher. Although he admits his act and his shame, she refuses to hear *his* confession of his past and leaves. At the end of the semester Cronin, wretched with a sense of his unworthiness, returns to Chicago. A year later he receives a card from Mary Lou which states she is still in college and hopes "someday to teach" (87).

Oddly enough, for all the dangers that beset the theme of the redeemed prostitute, "A Choice of Profession" works. Despite the elaborate mythic machinery, the story achieves a grimly realistic intensity; and if Cronin never comes alive beyond his function, Mary Lou does. Perhaps the only legitimate reservation the reader can have is that the story is "heavy-handed"—that behind the action there is less inspiration than outline.

IX *New Techniques*

Fortunately, however, the story does not end the collection. Two other tales, and these among the most recent Malamud has done, remain to be discussed; and both of them herald a striking departure from the earlier work. "Black is My Favorite Color" and "The German Refugee" return to a favorite setting, New York City; both are concerned with Jews under the stress of guilt; and both are about the terror of masks and of love corrupted. The ingredients, in other words, are the same as those which made up the better stories in the earlier collection. However, in both cases the resemblance to past stories is only slight, and in reading them one senses a whole new direction as well as an entirely different sense of reality.

Perhaps the element most notably absent from these stories is fantasy. In both, Malamud seems to be pitting his vision against a firmer reality, to be working with objective experience in a way he had never before done. The most important sign of this approach is that his own presence in the stories is absent. The two pieces represent the first time in his writing career that he has entirely forsaken the omniscient point of view. Both stories are told through a first-person narrator—one, in fact, is a monologue—and by virtue of this technique the author has automatically divested the stories of the most persuasive though most elusive element in his Jewish tales—the sense of his own mitigating compassion.

This latter fact is especially true of the longest of the two stories, "The German Refugee" (1963), which is told by a twenty-year-old college student who has been hired to teach English to a middle-aged refugee from Hitler's Germany. Moreover, the refugee, Oskar Gassner, is totally unlike the refugees in *The Magic Barrel*. An intellectual writer and critic, Gassner is one of the great men of the world who have fled the incinerators of the old country to take their chances in America. Indeed, in framing his story about this new kind of refugee, Malamud has also broadened it—for the first time in any of his shorter works—to a full and overt sense of the world at large. The problems of world-wide insecurity and inhumanity parallel, and in time dove-tail neatly, with the personal wound that lies at the heart of Oskar Gassner's character. Apparently like the Fascists, Gassner is riding the crest of an awful death wish. Having willfully left his Gentile wife of twenty-seven years in Europe—along with his anti-Semitic mother-in-law—Gassner must tend the twin sorrows of alienation and a sense of personal unworthiness. Unable, because unwilling, to learn English, he has succumbed to a paralysis of the will. But, since his survival in America depends upon his ability to deliver in the fall a lecture for the Institute for Public Studies, Gassner has called in the narrator, Martin Goldberg, who through a blistering summer attempts, first optimistically and then by an act of despairing sympathy, to teach the despondent refugee the intricacies of the unfamiliar tongue.

In time, with the language at least, Goldberg succeeds. The lecture, however, is something else. Though he begins it a dozen times, Gassner can never get beyond the first page, and he vows, "If I do not this legture prepare, I will take my life" (202). The pronouncement rides ceaselessly over the dark encroachment of two separate but interrelated leitmotives: the Nazi-Soviet Pact and Gassner's perpetual torment because of the wife he has left behind.

That Malamud is trying to connect the two strands seems clear. The general failure of humanity—the shadow of genocide and hate as a generalized death wish—is bound up and particularized in Oskar Gassner's guilt for his actions toward his wife. Yearning for death, the refugee finds himself in dreams identifying with the Nazis and the forces of anti-life generally. The problem is rooted in some failure or corruption of love; and its corrective lies in a sudden affirmation of love through an act of love.

The agent who brings about Oskar Gassner's temporary salvation is the narrator himself, whose faith in the old refugee carries him to the library where he reads about Gassner's subject: the influence of Whitman on German literature. When Martin takes his notes to Gassner, the ensuing scene suddenly rights an elemental wrong. Listening with sadness to Martin's ideas, Gassner suddenly rouses himself: ". . . no, it wasn't the love of death they got from Whitman—that ran through German poetry—but it was most of all his feeling for Brudermensch, his humanity. . . . But this does not grow long on German earth . . ." (209).

Gassner's pronouncement, in effect an affirmation of life through love, prompts him to complete the lecture. In the fall, with the coming of cooler weather, he delivers it without flaw, reading the words as if they were a screen against the world's impending catastrophe. Warsaw has just fallen, but the words of the poem rise bravely:

> And I know that the spirit of God is the brother of my own,
> And that all the men ever born are also my brothers, and the
>   women my sisters and lovers,
> And that the kelson of creation is love, . . .

This quotation is the limit of the story's affirmation. The theme of realization too late, a theme that haunts so many of the earlier stories, again is given the last word. Here perhaps there is more reason than ever before, for the worst barbarity of history is simply too monstrous to be mitigated. Two days after the lecture, Martin returns to Gassner's apartment to find the old man a suicide. Later, he discovers the cause in a letter sent to the refugee "by his anti-semitic mother-in-law":

> She writes in a tight script it takes me hours to decipher, that her daughter, after Oskar abandons her, against her own mother's fervent pleas and anguish, is converted to Judaism by a vengeful rabbi. One night the Brown Shirts appear, and though the mother wildly waves her bronze crucifix in their faces, they drag Frau Gassner, together with the other Jews, out of the apartment house, and transport them in lorries to a small border town in conquered Poland. There, it is rumored, she is shot in the head and topples into an open tank ditch, with the naked Jewish men, their wives and children, some Polish soldiers, and a handful of Gypsies. (212)

"The German Refugee" is assuredly Malamud's most ambitious as well as his saddest story. Not only does it provide a new "method" but it also replaces the insulated settings of the earlier tales with a concrete social canvas. Moreover, the transition involves a larger, more intricate structure than any of the previous stories. For this reason one is tempted to overrate the attempt at the expense of the actual response. But even if it is not one of Malamud's most realized stories, "The German Refugee" is still impressive, especially in its effort to balance large social issues on the slender strand of individual torment. If Martin Goldberg's vision does not really support the use of the first-person narrator, the alteration of method has supplied the author with dramatic possibilities he has never before employed and which, on the whole, he has used to good effect. Perhaps most importantly, this story has opened up new fictional possibilities.

That Malamud can take full advantage of these possibilities is amply demonstrated by "Black is My Favorite Color" (1963), which is not only one of the best stories in the entire collection but one which deserves to stand with some of the finer pieces in *The Magic Barrel.* At once comic and terrifying, the story again involves the author in the problem of racial antagonisms and, for the first time since "Angel Levine," in the specific problems of Jewish-Negro relations. The story, however, is not a fantasy; and the narrator, Nat Lime, a naïve liquor store owner of "forty-four, a bachelor with a daily growing bald spot," is no angel-encountering Jobian tailor. Instead, Nat is a victim amid victims, whose special fate as a boy and as a man, is to bang his balding head against the facts of blackness. Black "is still my favorite color," Nat says in the opening; but he can add, "you wouldn't know it from my luck" (88).

What animates and reveals the story is Nat Lime's magical voice, picking its way between knowledge and ignorance, vulgarity and saintliness, with almost acrobatic skill. At times, in his despair over the failure of communion, he can sound like Frankie Alpine bewailing the impossibility to communicate through the baffling screen of misunderstanding: "If they knew what was in my heart towards them, but how can you tell that to anybody nowadays? I've tried more than once but the language of the heart either is a dead language or else nobody understands it the way you speak it" (18). At other times he can sound like an aggressive Frankie nursing his failure in a self-pity that hides hostility: "That's how it is. I give my heart and they kick me in the teeth" (30).

Ostensibly, the "kicks in the teeth" dominate the story, both in the recounting of Nat's early and later life. There was, first, Buster Wilson, the Negro boy who had accepted from young Nat such tokens of friendship as money and candy only to turn on him unexpectedly and scream: "Take your Jew movies and your Jew candy and shove them up your Jew ass" (22). Later, there had been the Negress, Ornita, whom he had loved and then lost on a cold February night when a group of Negroes had accosted them in the street and assailed Nat as a "Jewish landlord" and Ornita as a traitor. Presently there is Charity Sweetness, the cleaning lady from Father Divine's who refuses to eat her lunch at Nat's table but, with a distant smile on her face, retreats to the bathroom and locks the door.

In this regard—as a story of love and friendship defeated by the world—"Black is My Favorite Color" could hardly be better, nor its sense of reality more persuasive. However, this is only one aspect of the story, and in some ways the least important. The full measure of Nat's frustration lies less in the collision of self and the world than in the collision within Nat himself. Like Frankie Alpine, Nat in effect speaks two tongues, and his motivations persistently double back in a dialogue in which good and bad, the *mensch* and the non-*mensch* collide. To Ornita's apprehensive "What about children? Were you looking forward to half-Jewish polka dots?" he can reply, in an echo of Frankie's admonishment to Helen's talk of Jewishness, "I was looking forward to children" (27). But at another point, describing Ornita, he can say: "Her face was pretty, with big eyes and high cheek bones, but lips a little thick and nose a little broad" (24). Such disparate reactions, as well as Nat's consummately fractured gestures and intonations, dramatize the narrator's dilemma. As with all of Malamud's heroes, Nat's problem with self-integration is the crucial one. But the drama is compounded by the nature of the subject, and particularly by Nat's lack of insight, into a story more ambiguous and perhaps more agonized than most. Moreover, Malamud's irony is unrelenting, for Nat's human assaults on the barriers which separate him from self as well as from Negroes persistently turn rank in the noses of those who receive them. In effect, Malamud is saying that even the gestures of good carry their own peril in the real world. Altogether, the story could not be more baffling, nor, for this very reason, more convincing. In the conclusion there remains only the awful scene: the divided victim, a poor benighted Everyman, alone in his kitchen unavailingly screaming for a way through the barriers that deprive him of communion: "Charity Sweetness—You hear me?—Come out of that goddamn toilet!" (30).

CHAPTER *6*

Conclusion

A FRAGMENT from a play which Malamud is currently completing provides *Idiots First* with something of a bonus.
Entitled *Suppose A Wedding*, it apparently concerns the marital
and parental problems of a former actor in the Yiddish theater.
Not enough of it has been printed to warrant any comment,
but its presence is teasing—for it suggests that the author's experiments with prose fiction have perhaps momentarily en-
countered a blind alley—and reassuring since it attests to the
author's continuing vitality. And it must be said that whatever
reassurance the play offers is deeply needed. For despite some
of the advances represented by the last few stories considered,
Idiots First clearly represents a decline from Malamud's earlier
achievements. Compared to the impact of *The Magic Barrel*, in
fact, it seems flat, repetitious, and at times precariously strained.

I Idiots First *compared to* The Magic Barrel

In some ways, of course, such a reaction to *Idiots First* could
not be otherwise. Insofar as the collection recapitulates many
of the concerns of the first one, it would be presumptuous to
expect the novelty of *The Magic Barrel*. However, it is also
true that any realized work of art creates its own novelty; and
this most of the tales in *Idiots First* do not do. If the burdens
imposed on the central characters remain constant—and, at
times, are even heavier—few of the later stories manage to evoke
that luminous, distinctive sense of redemptive suffering that
Malamud created again and again in the earlier fables. In trying to reach for "more of the world," he seems to have lost that
special province which, while small, turned *The Magic Barrel*
into one of the most exciting literary achievements of the last

decade. Spare as the earlier stories are, the author yet managed to consolidate in them the real and the fantastic in a totally novel style—a mixture of chant, roguishness, and despair (the occasional clumsiness of which was, as Randall Jarrell once said of a modern poet, "a guarantee of truth"[1]); and more, he managed through that style to create spiritual possibilities out of the debris of victimization.

No doubt, his earlier achievement demanded in part that the author disregard, as Norman Podhoretz has suggested, the full range of "historical currents in which the rest of us are being swept away."[2] But it was only by some such willful reduction that Malamud could perfect his vision. In his last work, however, he has attempted to extend his talents into areas too large to accommodate his special vision, and the same impulses that mar *A New Life* also mar *Idiots First*. The energetic absurdities of "Still Life" and "Naked Nude," as well as the attenuated symbolism of the title story, are in part a frustrated recoil from the difficulty of his task.

II *Malamud's Literary Progress*

If *Idiots First* can be said to "serve" at all, it is perhaps as a kind of way station by which to identify Malamud's present and future direction. If it does nothing more, the collection demonstrates the continuation of a line of development already suggested by the progress of his earliest work. Both as a novelist and a short story writer he has repeatedly demonstrated a dedication to his craft that is almost as rare as his gifts. He is a writer—odd enough in our day—who takes chances. In every case, moreover, the risks are taken in an effort to rescue man from an Underground which has for too long been cultivated as the only means of identifying him as Man. For all its failings, *Idiots First* establishes Malamud as a member of that select company of contemporary writers who are seeking, as Jack Ludwig recently wrote, to liberate fiction "from the tyranny of symbolic smallness . . . to catch the visible world in all its complexity, clangor, and untriumphant celebration."[3]

Needless to say, it is difficult to decipher an author's motivation; but it seems that the changes in Malamud's fiction, particularly his attempt to carry his affirmative dialogue into a more direct confrontation with the world, are inseparable from his own honesty. In one of his few public pronouncements, Malamud said of a former teacher, Theodore Goodman, that "He taught me to beware of being dishonest as a writer. He said to me: 'Either you go in honest, or you sink.' And I've tried to stick to that ever since."[4] By and large, Malamud *has* stuck to that principle, even if it has meant extending himself beyond the resources of his talent. In innumerable ways the development of his three novels and his stories mirror an author who seems to be defining himself anew with each work. If *The Natural* appeared, as it did to many critics, one of the most original novels of its day, it nonetheless presents a very doubtful introduction to the author of *The Assistant*. And while *The Assistant* continues to be accounted among the *best* novels of the decade, it is at best only a dubious overture to *A New Life*.

Each of these works represents not just a re-elaboration of theme but, in some ways, an entire alteration of manner. With *The Natural* Malamud wrote a novel which represents at one and the same time an excursion into hallucination and a poetic investigation of some of the distinctive sources of modern anxiety. In its meld of farce and seriousness, myth and baseball, all of which is held together by an extraordinary coupling of lyrical symbolism and jargon, he created a work which may hide the seriousness of its intent under a contagious and pleasurable comedy, but which nonetheless bears out Leslie Fiedler's contention that "the modern instance and the remembered myth are equally felt, equally realized and equally appropriate to our predicament."

But, as Fiedler added, Malamud managed this success only by working within a method in which he "has not felt obliged to choose between the richness of imagined detail and that of symbolic relevance. He is out of the trap!"[5] To be out of the trap, however, is a trick of craft and hardly a moral victory; and this fact Malamud has realized. For in his second and better novel, only traces of the mythic manner of the first work remain. The ritual cycle of Roy Hobbes's career is, with the history of Frankie Alpine, submerged—though not obliterated—in a sad and realistic evocation of frustration and hope that conflicts on every level with the myth itself and so transforms *The Assistant* into a work that seems to have no precedent in recent literature. It can be said of it, as the judges who awarded *The Magic Barrel* the National Book Award said of that work, that "it captures the poetry of human relations at the point where imagination and reality meet."[6] Ambivalent from first to last, undercut by currents of ritual and realism, *The Assistant* seems to belong to no convention unless it be to Dostoevsky's fiercely visionary "extra-realism." Or perhaps one may assign it to the tradition of Yiddish irony—the kind of irony, as Earl Rovit has put it, which "values one's self and mankind as both less and more than they seem to be worth."[7] Assuredly, it is only in some such confused but intensely human vision—its logical untidiness the very center of its persuasiveness—that one can account for the inexplicable power of the novel.

If the alteration of manner which marks the transition from *The Natural* to *The Assistant* suggests that the impulses which underlie Malamud's experiments with craft are rooted in his own integrity, *A New Life* suggests that this integrity is inviolable. Where *The Assistant* places the purely psychological drama of *The Natural* in a far more real arena, *A New Life*, the last of the novels, lies exposed to the attack of an "actual" present. The largest and the most complex of the novels, *A New Life* is also Malamud's most realistic work. Not only does it investigate the cycle of redemption basic to the earlier novels, but it seeks also to extend that analysis into heretofore untapped areas of experience.

Moreover, the same progress, though to a less spectacular degree, is also true in the stories. Though the tales in *The Magic Barrel* share something of the tradition of European Yiddish storytelling, moderated and reinforced by Malamud's own rigorous intellectual and literary concerns, the collection is filled with some of the same disparities of manner observed in the novels. In the tales that deal with the young, or those which deal with the American in Europe, but particularly in the later tales in *Idiots First,* Malamud seemingly is seeking diversity not for novelty but in order to enlarge his themes—to find the means for allowing his characters to breathe above ground. In the process, and no matter the failings involved, he is also attempting to discover the way to bring into his fiction something of the breadth and vigor one finds in the literature of an earlier day. If only unconsciously, he is striving to break through what Irving Howe has described as one of the most pressing difficulties faced by the serious writer of "post-modern fiction": the amorphous, unsettled state of the present affluent and passivity-ridden society which denies the novelist what was in the past his richest resource—the drama of the individual self in collision with a clear social reality.

Much of Malamud's work bears the imprint of that difficulty, particularly his early and late symbolist work, but also his fiction of the mid-1950's. In seeking to create in *The Assistant*—as well as in many of the short stories—a kind of Dostoevskian drama, he has erected settings that are, for all their stench of realism, metaphors—eternal ghettos—exactly such settings, as Howe puts it, which are intended to "recapture intensities of feeling we have apparently lost but take to be characteristic of an earlier decade."[8] But in his later work—in *A New Life* and in the most recent stories—Malamud has sought for a way out of this limitation, for the frames by which he might cope with larger areas of reality and yet retain the "intensities" of his earlier work. In this attempt he has failed, for it has meant forgoing the kind of materials he instinctively handles to best advantage. He has, in fact, gambled with his art.

However, failure is a relative term. If the later works lack the power of the earlier, many of them are more than promising. Honesty in literature is no guarantee of success; but it is an indispensable ingredient in any success. What is most noteworthy about such stories as "The German Refugee" or "Black is My Favorite Color" is that they manage dramatically to extend the author's range with only a small diminution of power. If they do not yet possess the force and magic of his best work, it is only because some more powerful alchemy must be found to banish material demons—and because, finally, it is difficult to find *anywhere* in current literature the stories or the novels that one might place alongside Malamud's finest.

Ultimately, this last consideration must be paramount in any discussion of Malamud's career to date. Although the play he is currently working on may indicate a frustration in the search for new literary modes instead of a promising new beginning, he has already amply justified most of our legitimate expectations for a major writer. In such stories as "The Loan" or "The

Last Mohican" and preeminently in "The Magic Barrel," he has created works which are as convincing as they are uncanny; and in his second novel, *The Assistant,* he has written not only one of the best novels of recent years but perhaps the *very* best. If he has avoided in these works certain of those "corrosive currents" which blight the search for affirmation, he has never denied the elements of spiritual despair, of human isolation, of love corrupted and "goodness" infected which as often as not overwhelms the agents of redemption. In all his better work his pessimism as much as anything else makes his tales of redemption persuasive. For it is against this pessimism that his most realized characters must contend if they are to demonstrate that man's capacity for renewal is not to be denied by a mere summary of his ailments. Perhaps Norman Podhoretz best described Malamud's achievement in this regard when he wrote of the author: "His work, when it is good—which sufficiently often it is—seems a kind of miracle, an act of spiritual autonomy perfect enough to persuade us that the possibility of freedom from the determinings of history and sociology still exists."[9]

Although Malamud's career seems only to be beginning and already to be entering new channels, he has succeeded in bringing to American literature a note that has long been absent from it, and in a style it never possessed. In a period when the novel itself threatens to vanish under the weight of anti-novels and anti-heroes, when denigration and nihilism have become the norm, Malamud has dedicated himself to tending the resources of human personality which seem to be disappearing not just from literature but from life itself. "Our most important natural resource is Man," the author has said;[10] and in full and open conflict with his own despair, he has created works which prove the point. Despite the evidence of his and our senses, he manages to affirm man, to find the vision through which the elusive and enigmatic sense of life's possibilities counters (all reality to the contrary) man's fall from grace. Through his portrait of a people engulfed and tortured by barbarities past and present, he has found the means to regain something of the tragic vision of the past which insists that where there is no hope man will continue to hope, where the spirit cannot endure it will continue to endure.

Notes and References

Chapter One

1. Quoted in Joseph Wershba, "Not Horror but 'Sadness,' " New York *Post*, September 14, 1958, p. M2.
2. Leslie Fiedler, "The Jew as Mythic American," *Ramparts,* II (Autumn, 1963), 32.
3. Ihab Hassan, *Radical Innocence: Studies in the Contemporary American Novel* (Princeton, 1961), p. 161.
4. Quoted in Wershba, *op. cit.,* p. M2.
5. Isaac Rosenfeld, *An Age of Enormity* (Cleveland, 1962), p. 63.
6. *Ibid.,* p. 69.
7. Leslie Fiedler, *The Jew in the American Novel* (New York, 1959), p. 5.
8. Lionel Trilling, *Freud and the Crisis of Our Culture* (Boston, 1955), p. 58.
9. Reprinted in Granville Hicks, "Literary Horizons," *Saturday Review of Literature* (October 12, 1963), 32.
10. Hassan, *op. cit.,* p. 11.
11. Franz Kafka, *The Diaries* (New York, 1948) I, 11.
12. Marcus Klein, *After Alienation: American Novels in Mid-Century* (Cleveland, 1964), p. 248.
13. Rosenfeld, *op. cit.,* p. 72.

Chapter Two

1. Joseph Campbell, *The Hero with a Thousand Faces* (New York: Meridian Books, 1956), p. 217.
2. *The Creative Present,* ed. Nona Balakian and Charles Simmons (New York, 1963), p. 219.
3. Alfred Kazin, *Contemporaries* (Boston, 1962), p. 204.
4. Klein, *op. cit.,* p. 255.
5. Hassan, *op. cit.,* p. 161.
6. "I considered Judaism, once I got to know about it through reading, as another source of humanism. The first being Western literature and history from the Greeks on." Malamud to Richman, May 12, 1963.
7. *The Natural* (New York, 1952), p. 236. All subsequent page references are to this edition.
8. Jonathan Baumbach, "The Economy of Love: The Novels of Bernard Malamud," *The Kenyon Review,* XXV (Summer, 1963), 440.

9. Jessie Weston, *From Ritual to Romance* (New York: Anchor Books, 1957), p. 12.

10. Campbell, *op. cit.*, p. 101.

11. *Ibid.*, pp. 114-16.

12. Frank Kermode, "Bernard Malamud," *New Statesman* (March 30, 1962), 452.

13. Baumbach, *op. cit.*, p. 439.

14. Fiedler, *The Jew in the American Novel*, p. 57.

15. C. G. Jung, *Psyche and Symbol* (New York: Anchor Books, 1958), p. 130.

16. Malamud to Richman, May 12, 1963.

17. Ben Siegel, "Victims in Motion: Bernard Malamud's Sad and Bitter Clowns," reprinted in *Recent American Fiction: Some Critical Views*, ed. Joseph J. Waldmeir (Boston, 1963), p. 204.

18. *Esquire*, LX (July, 1963), 6.

19. Alfred Kazin, "Fantasist of the Ordinary," *Commentary*, XXIV (July, 1957), 90.

20. Siegel, *op. cit.*, p. 204.

Chapter Three

1. Martin Buber, *I and Thou* (New York: Scribner Library Books, 1958), p. 15.

2. Quoted in Hicks, *op. cit.*, p. 32.

3. *The Assistant* (New York, 1957), p. 10. All subsequent page references are to this edition.

4. Theodore Solotaroff, "Bernard Malamud's Fiction: The Old Life and the New," *Commentary*, III (March, 1962), 200.

5. Quoted in Wershba, *op. cit.*, p. M2.

6. *Ibid.*

7. Baumbach, *op. cit.*, p. 448.

8. Hassan, *op. cit.*, p. 164.

9. Solotaroff, *op. cit.*, p. 198.

10. Theodore Reik, *Jewish Wit* (New York: Gamut Books, 1962), p. 41.

11. *Ibid.*

12. Rosenfeld, *op. cit.*, p. 73.

13. Solotaroff, *op. cit.*, p. 198.

14. André Schwarz-Bart, *The Last of the Just* (New York, 1961), pp. 4-5.

15. Reik, *op. cit.*, p. 222.

16. Malcolm Diamond, *Martin Buber: Jewish Existentialist* (New York, 1960), pp. 110-37.

17. Malamud has said: "Italians and Jews are closely related in their consciousness of the importance of personality, in their emphasis on the richness of life, in their tremendous sense of past and tradition." Quoted in Wershba, *op. cit.*, p. M2.

18. Malamud is perhaps echoing in this regard Dostoevsky's concept of "higher realism."

19. Hassan, *op. cit.*, p. 168.

20. Cited in Diamond, *op. cit.*, p. 89.

21. Baumbach, *op. cit.*, p. 448.

22. Saul Bellow, *Recent American Fiction* (Washington: The Library of Congress, 1963), p. 12.

23. Richard Sewell, *The Vision of Tragedy* (New Haven, 1959), p. 8.

Chapter Four

1. *The Assistant*, p. 132.

2. Kazin, "Fantasist of the Ordinary," p. 90.

3. Philip Roth, "Writing American Fiction," *Commentary*, XXXI (March, 1961), 229.

4. Klein, *op. cit.*, p. 281.

5. *A New Life* (New York, 1961), p. 95. All subsequent page references are to this edition.

6. Quoted in Wershba, *op. cit.*, p. M2.

7. Klein, *op. cit.*, p. 282.

8. Eugene Goodheart, "Fantasy and Reality," *Midstream*, VII (Autumn, 1961), 104.

9. Solotaroff, *op. cit.*, p. 203.

10. Quoted in Wershba, *op. cit.*, p. M2.

11. Klein, *op. cit.*, p. 265.

12. Baumbach, *op. cit.*, p. 440.

13. Kermode, *op. cit.*, p. 453.

14. Solotaroff, *op. cit.*, p. 203.

15. Klein, *op. cit.*, pp. 291-92.

16. Solotaroff, *op. cit.*, p. 203.

17. Baumbach, *op. cit.*, p. 440.

18. Norman Podhoretz, "The New Nihilism in the American Novel," *Partisan Review*, XXV (Fall, 1958), 590.

Chapter Five

1. Quoted in Francis Brown, "It's Been a Pretty Good Year," New York *Times Book Review*, September 2, 1963, p. 3.

2. *The Magic Barrel* (New York, 1958), p. 3. All subsequent page references are to this edition.

3. Podhoretz, *op. cit.*, p. 589.

4. Earl Rovit, "Bernard Malamud and the Jewish Literary Tradition," *Critique*, III (Winter-Spring, 1960), 5.

5. Podhoretz, *op. cit.*, p. 589.

6. Dan Jacobson, "Magic and Morality," *Commentary*, XXVI (October, 1958), 360.

7. Alfred Kazin, "The Alone Generation," reprinted in *Recent American Fiction: Some Critical Views,* ed. Joseph J. Waldmeir (Boston, 1963), p. 10.

8. *Idiots First* (New York, 1964), p. 3. All subsequent page references are to this edition.

Chapter Six

1. Randall Jarrell, *Poetry and the Age* (New York: Vintage Books, 1955), p. 151.

2. Podhoretz, *op. cit.*, p. 590.

3. Jack Ludwig, *Recent American Novelists* (Minnesota, 1962), p. 42.

4. Quoted in Wershba, *op. cit.*, p. M2.

5. Leslie Fiedler, "In the Interest of Surprise and Delight," *Folio,* XX (Summer, 1955), 20.

6. Reprinted in Hicks, *op. cit.*, p. 32.

7. Rovit, *op. cit.*, p. 32.

8. Irving Howe, "Mass Society and Post-Modern Fiction," *Partisan Review,* XXVI (Summer, 1959), 432.

9. Podhoretz, *op. cit.*, p. 590.

10. Hicks, *op. cit.*, p. 32.

Selected Bibliography

PRIMARY SOURCES

The Natural. New York: Harcourt, Brace and Company, Inc., 1952.
The Assistant. New York: Farrar, Straus and Company, Inc., 1957.
The Magic Barrel. New York: Farrar, Straus and Company, Inc., 1958.
A New Life. New York: Farrar, Straus and Company, Inc., 1961.
Idiots First. New York: Farrar, Straus and Company, Inc., 1963.

SECONDARY SOURCES

1. *Biographical Sources*

CADLE, DEAN. "Bernard Malamud," *Wilson Library Bulletin,* XXXIII (December, 1958), 226. Reprinted in *Current Biography Yearbook.* New York: H. H. Wilson Co., 1958.

WERSHBA, JOSEPH. "Not Horror but 'Sadness,'" New York *Post,* September 14, 1958, p. M2.

2. *Studies of Malamud*

While the author is noted in most discussions of contemporary fiction, there are few extended studies of Malamud. The following items were judged the most valuable.

BAUMBACH, JONATHAN. "The Economy of Love: The Novels of Bernard Malamud," *The Kenyon Review,* XXV (Summer, 1963), 438-57. One of the best and most comprehensive studies of Malamud's novels. Especially valuable for tracing the uses of love in the three novels. Contains also an excellent analysis of the mythic structure of *The Natural.*

BLUEFARB, SAM. "Bernard Malamud: The Scope of Caricature," *English Journal,* XXIII (July, 1964), 319-26. Sees patterns of traditional allegory in many of Malamud's characters.

FIEDLER, LESLIE. *The Jew in the American Novel.* New York: Herzl Institute Pamphlet, 1959. A brief attempt to place Malamud's fiction in the context of the history of the Jew in American literature.

————. *No! in Thunder.* Boston: Beacon Press, 1960. A discussion of *The Natural* and *The Assistant* which contains valuable comments on the uniqueness of both.

Selected Bibliography

Hassan, Ihab. *Radical Innocence: Studies in the Contemporary American Novel.* Princeton: Princeton University Press, 1961. A lengthy discussion of *The Assistant* which is particularly provocative for its comments on Morris Bober and on the ambiguities within the novel.

Hicks, Granville. "Bernard Malamud," *The Creative Present,* ed. Nona Balakian and Charles Simmons. New York: Doubleday, 1963. An attempt to distinguish the general patterns in all of Malamud's fiction.

Hoyt, Charles A. "Bernard Malamud and the New Romanticism," *Contemporary American Novelists,* ed. Harry T. Moore. Carbondale: Southern Illinois University Press, 1964. An interesting attempt to define the novels in terms of romantic values.

Kazin, Alfred. *Contemporaries.* Boston: Little, Brown, 1962. Brief but illuminating discussion of Malamud's relationship to the European Yiddish realists. Excellent for its analysis of the distinctive qualities of the Jewish materials.

Kermode, Frank. "Bernard Malamud," *New Statesman* (March 30, 1962), 452-53. An incisive treatment of the interrelated themes of the three novels.

Klein, Marcus. *After Alienation: American Novels in Mid-Century.* Cleveland: World Publishing Co., 1964. One of the most perceptive and thorough investigations of Malamud's novels. Especially good in its analysis of the foundations of his values, and for tracing the patterns of the author's thought back to two early, uncollected short stories.

Leer, Norman. "Three American Novels and Contemporary Society: A Search for Commitment," *Wisconsin Studies in Contemporary Literature,* III (Fall, 1962), 67-85. A good discussion of the role of the environment in *The Assistant* and the relationship of the novel to literary problems raised by the state of contemporary society.

Ludwig, Jack. *Recent American Novelists.* Minnesota: University of Minnesota Pamphlet on American Writers, 1962. Places Malamud in the context of the contemporary American novel.

Podhoretz, Norman. "The New Nihilism in the American Novel," *Partisan Review,* XXV (Fall, 1958), 589-90. While short, it throws a good deal of light on the dramatic power of Malamud's themes—particularly as presented in the short stories.

Ratner, Marc L. "Style and Humanity in Malamud's Fiction," *Massachusetts Review,* V (Summer, 1964), 663-83. Interesting, thorough discussion of Malamud's style.

Rovit, Earl H. "Bernard Malamud and the Jewish Literary Tradition," *Critique,* III (Winter-Spring, 1960), 3-10. Probably the best discussion of Malamud's short stories as they pertain to the Jewish literary tradition.

SIEGEL, BEN. "Victims in Motion: Bernard Malamud's Sad and Bitter Clowns," *Northwest Review*, V (Spring, 1962), 69-80. A fine treatment of *The Natural, The Assistant,* and *The Magic Barrel,* with special emphasis on the nature of the heroes in these works.

SOLOTAROFF, THEODORE. "Bernard Malamud's Fiction: The Old Life and the New," *Commentary*, III (March, 1962), 197-204. Special emphasis given to the difficulties Malamud faced in extending his distinctive materials in *A New Life*. Contains valuable insights into all three novels.

3. *Selected Reviews*

The Natural

FIEDLER, LESLIE. "In the Interest of Surprise and Delight," *Folio*, XX (Summer, 1955), 17-20. High praise and a thoughtful analysis of the relevance of the baseball hero to contemporary issues.

PODHORETZ, NORMAN. "Achilles in Left Field," *Commentary*, XV (March, 1953), 321-26. An early but thorough analysis of the mythic structure of *The Natural*. Contains important information on the parallels to *The Iliad*.

The Assistant

BAILEY, ANTHONY. "Insidious Patience," *Commonweal*, LXVI (June 21, 1957), 307-8. Perceptive comments on the concluding sections of the novel.

FRANCIS, H. E. "Bernard Malamud's Everyman," *Midstream*, VII (Winter, 1961), 93-97. A solid discussion of the style.

KAZIN, ALFRED. "Fantasist of the Ordinary," *Commentary*, XXIV (July, 1957), 89-92. Interesting criticism of Malamud's "unnecessary" symbolism.

SWADOS, HARVEY. "The Emergence of an Artist," *Western Review*, XXII (Winter, 1958), 149-51. A highly appreciative study of the originality of the book.

The Magic Barrel

JACOBSON, DAN. "Magic and Morality," *Commentary*, XXIV (October, 1958), 359-61. Perceptive comments on Malamud's use of the cadences of Yiddish speech.

POPKIN, HENRY. "Jewish Stories," *Kenyon Review*, XX (Autumn, 1958), 637-41. Excellent summary of the major tensions in the stories.

A New Life

GOODHEART, EUGENE. "Fantasy and Reality," *Midstream*, VII (Autumn, 1961), 102-5. Especially valuable analysis of Malamud's possible indebtedness to Tolstoy.

HYMAN, STANLEY EDGARD. "A New Life for a Good Man." Reprinted in *On Contemporary Literature*, ed. RICHARD KOSTELANETZ. New York: Avon Books, 1964. Highly appreciative review which sees the novel as a sign of Malamud's continuing growth.

HOLLANDER, JOHN. "To Find the Westward Path," *Partisan Review*, XXIX (Winter, 1962), 137-39. Interesting comment on the significance of the West in the novel.

Idiots First

LEIBOWITZ, HERBERT. "Malamud and the Anthropomorphic Business," *The New Republic*, C (December 21, 1963), 21-23. Especially good for the analysis of the Fidelman stories and "The German Refugee."

SOLOTAROFF, THEODORE. "Teaching Us what it Means: Human," *Book Week* (October 13, 1963), 5. Some contrast between the manner of the new and the early stories.

Index

Index